400-calorie
Mains

Paré • Billey • McLaren • Darcy

HEALTHY COOKING

400 Calorie Mains

First Printing February 2014
Library and Archives Canada Cataloguing in Publication
Paré, Jean, 1927-, author
400 calorie mains / Jean Paré, Sheridan McLaren, Ashley Billey.
(Healthy cooking series)
Includes index.
ISBN 978-1-927126-94-3 (pbk.)
1. Low-calorie diet--Recipes. 2. Cookbooks. I. McLaren, Sheridan, author II. Billey, Ashley, author III. Title. IV. Title: Four hundred calorie mains. V. Series: Healthy cooking (Company's Coming)
RM222.2.P365 2014   641.5'635   C2014-905083-6

Thanks to Sandy Weatherall of Jinsei Photographics for the food photograpy, to Ashley Billey for recipe prep and food styling, and to Sheridan Maclaren for the recipes on pages 50, 84 and 112; thanks also to Kseniya Ragozina / Photos.com for the photo on page 5, to ErnestoG / Photos.com for the photo on page 6 and to Lester120 / Thinkstock for the partial photo on the cover.

Published by
Company's Coming Publishing Limited
2311 – 96 Street NW
Edmonton, Alberta, Canada T6N 1G3
Tel: 780-450-6223   Fax: 780-450-1857
www.companyscoming.com

Company's Coming is a registered trademark owned by Company's Coming Publishing Limited

We acknowledge the financial support of the Government of Canada through the Canada Book Fund (CBF) for our publishing activities.

Printed in China

PC: 27

CONTENTS

The Company's Coming Story

Jean Paré (pronounced "jeen PAIR-ee") grew up understanding that the combination of family, friends and home cooking is the best recipe for a good life. When Jean left home, she took with her a love of cooking, many family recipes and an intriguing desire to read cookbooks as if they were novels!

When her four children had all reached school age, Jean volunteered to cater the 50th anniversary celebration of the Vermilion School of Agriculture, now Lakeland College, in Alberta, Canada. Working out of her home, Jean prepared a dinner for more than 1,000 people, launching a flourishing catering operation that continued for over 18 years.

"Never share a recipe you wouldn't use yourself."

As requests for her recipes increased, Jean was often asked the question, "Why don't you write a cookbook?" The publication of *150 Delicious Squares* on April 14, 1981 marked the debut of what would soon become one of the world's most popular cookbook series.

Company's Coming cookbooks are distributed in Canada, the United States, Australia and other world markets. Bestsellers many times over in English, Company's Coming cookbooks have also been published in French and Spanish.

Familiar and trusted in home kitchens around the world, Company's Coming cookbooks are offered in a variety of formats. Highly regarded as kitchen workbooks, the softcover Original Series, with its lay-flat plastic comb binding, is still a favourite among readers.

Jean Paré's approach to cooking has always called for *quick and easy recipes* using *everyday ingredients.* That view has served her well.

Jean continues to share what she calls The Golden Rule of Cooking: *Never share a recipe you wouldn't use yourself.* It's an approach that has worked—*millions of times over!*

Nutrition Information Guidelines

Each recipe is analyzed using the most current version of the Canadian Nutrient File from Health Canada, which is based on the United States Department of Agriculture (USDA) Nutrient Database.

- If more than one ingredient is listed (such as "butter or hard margarine"), or if a range is given (1 – 2 tsp., 5 – 10 mL), only the first ingredient or first amount is analyzed.

- For meat, poultry and fish, the serving size per person is based on the recommended 4 oz. (113 g) uncooked weight (without bone), which is 2 – 3 oz. (57 – 85 g) cooked weight (without bone)— approximately the size of a deck of playing cards.

- Milk used is 1% M.F. (milk fat), unless otherwise stated.

- Cooking oil used is canola oil, unless otherwise stated.

- Ingredients indicating "sprinkle," "optional," or "for garnish" are not included in the nutrition information.

- The fat in recipes and combination foods can vary greatly depending on the sources and types of fats used in each specific ingredient. For these reasons, the amount of saturated, monounsaturated and polyunsaturated fats may not add up to the total fat content.

Introduction

For many people, maintaining (or achieving) a healthy weight can be a challenge. The market is flooded with specialty diets, weight-loss programs, superfoods, gadgets, apps, books, DVDs and the like, all geared to help consumers reach or stay at their target weight. Some of these products may be helpful, others not so much, and a great deal of the information out there seems to be contradictory. But managing your weight doesn't need to be complicated. The bottom line is, to control your weight, you must control how many calories you eat.

Nutrition aside, it really doesn't matter how healthy the food you eat is if you eat too much of it. Calories are calories, and whether they come from vegetables, meat, grains or junkfood, they have the same function—to be burned as fuel for your body or reserved and stored as fat. For every 3500 calories you eat more than what your body burns, you gain 1 pound (454 grams) of fat; if you burn 3500 more calories than you take in, you lose 1 pound (454 grams) of fat. So the simplest way to maintain (or lose) weight is to balance the number of calories you ingest with what your body burns.

Dietary guidelines in Canada and the U.S. indicate that adult men need between 2500 and 3000 calories per day, depending on their age and activity level. For women, the numbers are a bit lower, between 1900 and 2400 calories per day. Your height and weight also help determine where you fall in that range.

Watching your calories doesn't have to mean depriving yourself of the foods you love; the key is a combination of making healthy food choices, portion control and moderation. Fat contains more than twice as many calories as carbohydrates or protein (9 calories in 1 gram of fat vs. 4 calories in 1 gram of protein or carbs), and 1 Tbsp (15 mL) of fat has about 120 calories. For the same number of calories, you could eat 4 cups (4 L) of broccoli or 17 cups (4.25 L) of spinach (not that you'd want to, but you get the point). To keep calories in check, limit the amount fat you consume. Sure, fat is flavour, but broth, lemon juice, fresh herbs and spices can also add flavour, with far fewer calories.

Protein and fibre keep you feeling fuller for longer than simple carbohydrates, so try to work them into every meal. Lean meats and legumes are good sources of protein, and for fibre, choose whole grains, vegetables and fruit.

Portion control plays a role in calorie counting, but that doesn't mean you have to walk away from your meal without satisfying your hunger. Portion sizes in North America have grown dramatically in the last few decades, and most of us now eat far more calories than we realize—or need. *In this book, we've kept the mains under 400 calories, which leaves you enough room to pair them with a low-calorie side and leave the table satiated. Use this pattern for your other meals in the day, and you should still have enough calories left for a few healthy snacks, too.*

Watching your calorie intake doesn't have to be difficult, it just requires a little planning—and *400 Calorie Mains* is just the tool to get you on your way!

Stuffed Roast Beef with Red Wine Sauce

Serves 12

A tender roast filled with a moist horseradish stuffing and served with a succulent wine sauce.

Stuffing

4 bacon slices, chopped

1 cup (250 mL) diced onion

2 cups (500 mL) fresh bread crumbs

1 Tbsp (15 mL) prepared horseradish

3 Tbsp (45 mL) chopped fresh parsley

1/4 tsp (1 mL) salt

pepper, sprinkle

3 lbs (1.4 kg) top sirloin roast

1 cup (250 mL) water

(see next page)

Stuffing: Cook bacon in frying pan on medium until browned but still soft. Remove to paper towel. Transfer to medium bowl. Drain and discard all but 1 Tbsp (15 mL) fat from pan.

Add onion. Cook on medium-low for about 10 minutes, stirring occasionally, until onion is soft. Add to bacon.

Add next 5 ingredients. Mix well. Makes 2 1/2 cups (625 mL) stuffing.

Cut deep horizontal pocket in side of roast almost through to other side. Fill with stuffing. Tie with butcher's string at 1 1/2 inch (3.8 cm) intervals. Place on greased wire rack in small roasting pan.

Pour water into bottom of pan. Cook roast, uncovered, in 425°F (220°C) oven for 25 minutes. Reduce heat to 350°F (175°C). Cook, uncovered, for about 1 hour until meat thermometer inserted into meat (not stuffing) reads 140°F (60°C) or until desired doneness. Remove to serving platter, leaving drippings in pan. Tent roast with foil. Let stand for 10 minutes. Carve into 1/4 inch (6 mm) thick slices.

Red Wine Sauce: Heat roasting pan drippings in small saucepan on medium-high. Add wine. Heat and stir for 5 to 7 minutes until reduced by half.

Combine remaining 6 ingredients in small bowl. Add to wine mixture. Heat and stir for about 5 minutes until jelly is liquid and sauce is thickened. Makes about 1 2/3 cups (400 mL) sauce. Serve with roast beef.

1 serving: 390 Calories; 19 g Total Fat (8 g Mono, 1 g Poly, 7 g Sat); 70 mg Cholesterol; 23 g Carbohydrate (less than 1 g Fibre, 6 g Sugar); 29 g Protein; 520 mg Sodium

Red Wine Sauce

1 cup (250 mL) dry red wine

1 cup (250 mL) prepared low-sodium beef broth

1/4 cup (60 mL) redcurrant jelly

1 1/2 Tbsp (22 mL) grainy mustard

1 Tbsp (15 mL) cornstarch

salt, sprinkle

pepper, sprinkle

Ruby-glazed Roast Beef

Serves 8

A beautifully done roast with the addition of a mild sweet glaze.

3 lbs (1.4 kg) inside round (or eye of round) roast

Place roast, fat side up, on rack in small roasting pan. Roast, uncovered, in 500°F (260°C) oven for 30 minutes. Reduce temperature to 275°F (140°C).

1 cup (250 mL) redcurrant jelly

1/2 tsp (2 mL) ground ginger

1/4 cup (60 mL) chopped sun-dried tomatoes, softened in boiling water for 10 minutes before chopping

1 tsp (5 mL) no-salt seasoning, Italian blend

Heat next 4 ingredients in small saucepan. Pour over roast. Roast, uncovered, for 25 minutes per lb (55 minutes per kg), basting several times with sauce, until meat thermometer registers 160°F (70°C) for medium. Transfer to cutting board. Tent with foil. Let stand for 10 minutes.

1/4 cup (60 mL) water

1 Tbsp (15 mL) cornstarch

Stir water into cornstarch in small cup until smooth. Gradually stir into juices in pan. Heat and stir until boiling and thickened. Serve with roast.

1 serving: 390 Calories; 13 g Total Fat (6 g Mono, 0.5 g Poly, 5 g Sat); 65 mg Cholesterol; 28 g Carbohydrate (0 g Fibre, 25 g Sugar); 38 g Protein; 140 mg Sodium

Spoon Beef and Mushroom Broth

Serves 4

Tender braised beef with edamame beans, a custom rice blend and a mighty mushroom broth to make this calorie-wise main course a great source of protein.

1 lb (454 g) top sirloin roast, trimmed of fat

1 Tbsp (15 mL) balsamic vinegar

1 Tbsp (15 mL) Dijon mustard

2 tsp (10 mL) canola oil

1/2 tsp (2 mL) paprika

1/4 tsp (1 mL) chopped fresh rosemary

1/4 tsp (1 mL) no-salt seasoning

1/2 tsp (2 mL) pepper

1 tsp (5 mL) canola oil

1/4 cup (60 mL) dry white wine

1 cup (250 mL) water

1/4 tsp (1 mL) salt

1 cup (250 mL) dried assorted mushrooms (chantrel, portobello, shitake, trumpet)

6 cups (1.5 L) water

(see next page)

Slice roast into 2 equal rectangular cuts, approximately 1 inch (2.5 cm) thick. Mix next 7 ingredients together in small bowl; pour into large resealable plastic bag. Add beef. Seal bag and turn to coat. Allow to marinate for at least 30 minutes.

Heat heavy-bottomed frying pan over high. Add second amount of canola oil followed by beef. Sear beef on all sides and transfer to roasting pan.

Deglaze frying pan with white wine, scraping away any bits stuck to bottom with a rubber spatula. Add first amount of water and salt. Pour liquid over beef. Cover. Cook in 300°F (150°C) oven for 3 to 4 hours, until meat is very tender. Remove from oven. Let stand in cooking liquid for 30 minutes.

While beef is roasting, combine dried mushrooms and second amount of water in large saucepan. Simmer on low for 1 hour. Strain off broth, reserving both liquid and mushrooms.

While broth is simmering, combine next 4 ingredients in small saucepan. Bring to a boil then reduce heat to low. Cover. Cook for 15 to 20 minutes until rice is done. Fluff with a fork.

To serve, place a portion of beef in the bottom of a warm bowl. Beside, add a spoonful of rice and some edmame beans, kale and reserved mushrooms together in a nest. Ladle mushroom broth around nest. Garnish with a dash of paprika.

1 serving: 400 Calories; 17 g Total Fat (8 g Mono, 2 g Poly, 5 g Sat); 60 mg Cholesterol; 25 g Carbohydrate (4 g Fibre, less than 1 g Sugar); 30 g Protein; 270 mg Sodium

Whole-grain rice mixtures can be found premixed at your local grocery store. Many contain an assortment of red and brown rice, and some even have quinoa. It is also quite simple to make your own custom mix. Simply choose an assortment of long-grain rice and quinoa from bulk bins and mix it together.

1/2 cup (125 mL) whole-grain rice mixture

l cup (250 mL) water

1/4 tsp (1 mL) no-salt seasoning

1/8 tsp (0.5 mL) cinnamon

1/2 cup (125 mL) fresh edamame beans, pods removed

1/2 cup (125 mL) baby kale

paprika, sprinkle

Beef and Pears in Wine

Serves 2

Tender, flavourful beef complemented by a fruity wine sauce. To ensure even cooking, remove beef from refrigerator 30 minutes before cooking. Serve with buttered pasta.

1/2–3/4 lb (225–340 g) beef tenderloin roast

1 tsp (5 mL) cooking oil

pepper, sprinkle

Place roast on greased wire rack in small roasting pan. Drizzle with first amount of cooking oil. Sprinkle with pepper. Cook, uncovered, in 350°F (175°C) oven for 40 to 45 minutes until meat thermometer reads 140°F (60°C) for medium doneness or until desired doneness. Transfer to cutting board. Tent with foil. Let stand for 10 minutes.

2 tsp (10 mL) cooking oil

2 Tbsp (30 mL) diced onion

Heat second amount of cooking oil in medium saucepan on medium-low. Add onion. Cook for about 5 minutes, stirring occasionally, until onion is soft.

1 cup (250 mL) dry red wine

2 Tbsp (30 mL) redcurrant jelly

2 tsp (10 mL) Dijon mustard

Add wine, jelly and mustard. Heat and stir on medium until jelly is liquid. Bring to a boil. Reduce heat to medium-low.

1 firm medium pear, peeled, cored and quartered

Add pear. Simmer, uncovered, for 10 to 15 minutes, stirring occasionally, until pear is soft. Remove pear. Keep warm. Strain wine mixture. Discard solids. Return wine mixture to same saucepan. Boil, uncovered, on medium-high for about 5 minutes, stirring occasionally, until thickened. Makes 1/3 cup (75 mL) sauce. Drizzle sauce over sliced beef and pear on individual plates.

1 serving: 390 Calories; 15 g Total Fat (7 g Mono, 2 g Poly, 3.5 g Sat); 55 mg Cholesterol; 18 g Carbohydrate (3 g Fibre, 9 g Sugar); 24 g Protein; 130 mg Sodium

Blue Cheese Beef Tenderloin

Serves 2

An instant classic. Bold flavours of creamy blue cheese and merlot-soaked beef tenderloin. A great shot of iron to give your metabolism a boost.

2 Tbsp (30 mL) dry red wine

1 Tbsp (15 mL) canola oil

1/2 tsp (2 mL) no-salt seasoning

1/2 tsp (2 mL) pepper

1/4 tsp (1 mL) chopped fresh rosemary

2 × 4 oz (113 g) beef tenderloin steaks (trimmed of fat), thick cut

2 oz (57 g) blue cheese

2 Tbsp (30 mL) milk

2 Tbsp (30 mL) fine dry bread crumbs (see Tip, page 86)

1/2 cup (125 mL) fresh spinach leaves

Mix together first 5 ingredients in small bowl. Pour marinade over steak in medium bowl and allow to marinate for at least 30 minutes.

In same small bowl from marinade, combine blue cheese, milk and bread crumbs. Work gently into a small, marbled ball. Cut ball in half and flatten each half onto parchment paper. Place in refrigerator until needed.

Heat cast iron pan over medium-high. Place each steak into hot pan. Sear steaks until bottoms are deep golden brown in colour, about 3 minutes. Flip steaks. Place flattened blue cheese slabs over each steak. Transfer entire pan to oven on bottom rack. Broil on high until cheese begins to bubble and develop a deep golden crust, about 3 to 5 minutes for medium-rare. If greater doneness is desired, bake steaks at 350°F (175°C) for a few more minutes. Remove from oven. Let stand for 5 minutes.

Serve hot over spinach.

1 serving: 380 Calories; 23 g Total Fat (9 g Mono, 2.5 g Poly, 9 g Sat); 80 mg Cholesterol; 7 g Carbohydrate (1 g Fibre, 1 g Sugar); 32 g Protein; 650 mg Sodium

Dark Mushroom Tenderloin

Serves 6

The rich-tasting sauce is flavoured with beer and earthy wild mushrooms. Serve with herbed potatoes and grilled zucchini.

1 1/2 Tbsp (22 mL) cooking oil

2 lbs (900 g) beef tenderloin roast

1/4 tsp (1 mL) no-salt seasoning, grilling blend

1/4 tsp (1 mL) pepper

Heat first amount of cooking oil in large frying pan on medium-high. Sprinkle roast with grilling seasoning and pepper. Add to frying pan. Cook for about 5 minutes, turning occasionally, until browned on all sides.

1 Tbsp (15 mL) Dijon mustard

2 cloves garlic, minced

1 tsp (5 mL) chopped fresh rosemary

Combine next 3 ingredients in small bowl. Brush over roast. Place on greased rack set in large baking sheet with sides. Cook in 425°F (220°C) oven for 15 minutes. Reduce heat to 350°F (175°C). Cook for about 45 minutes until internal temperature reaches 160°F (70°C) for medium or until roast reaches desired doneness. Transfer to cutting board. Tent with foil. Let stand for 10 minutes. Slice thinly.

1 × 12 oz (355 mL) bottle (or can) of dark beer (such as honey brown)

1 × 3/4 oz (22 g) package of dried porcini mushrooms

Bring beer to a boil in medium saucepan. Add porcini mushrooms. Stir. Remove from heat. Let stand, uncovered, for about 20 minutes until softened. Drain, reserving any remaining beer. Transfer to cutting board. Chop.

1 Tbsp (15 mL) cooking oil

1/2 cup (125 mL) diced onion

2 cups (500 mL) chopped fresh brown mushrooms

Heat second amount of cooking oil in large saucepan on medium-high. Add onion. Cook for about 3 minutes, stirring often, until softened. Add brown and porcini mushrooms. Reduce heat to medium. Cook for about 5 minutes, stirring often, until browned. Add reserved beer. Heat and stir, scraping any brown bits from bottom of pan, until boiling.

(see next page)

Stir broth into flour in small cup. Slowly add to mushroom mixture, stirring constantly until boiling and thickened.

Add cream. Stir. Serve with roast.

1 serving: *370 Calories; 19 g Total Fat (8 g Mono, 2 g Poly, 6 g Sat); 85 mg Cholesterol; 9 g Carbohydrate (1 g Fibre, 2 g Sugar); 35 g Protein; 240 mg Sodium*

1 cup (250 mL) prepared low-sodium beef broth

2 Tbsp (30 mL) all-purpose flour

1/2 cup (125 mL) half-and-half cream

Dijon-crusted Sirloin

Serves 4

For a great meal, bake some baby potatoes while you cook up this well-spiced steak.

1 Tbsp (15 mL) olive oil

1/4 cup (60 mL) thinly sliced green onion

1 clove garlic, minced

1/2 tsp (2 mL) dried oregano

1/2 tsp (2 mL) dried thyme

1/8 tsp (0.5 mL) salt

1/8 tsp (0.5 mL) pepper

1/8 tsp (0.5 mL) cayenne pepper

1/3 cup (75 mL) fine dry bread crumbs (see Tip, page 86)

3 Tbsp (45 mL) grated Parmesan cheese

2 tsp (10 mL) olive oil

1/2 tsp (2 mL) Montreal steak spice

1 lb (454 g) beef top sirloin steak

2 Tbsp (30 mL) Dijon mustard

2 Tbsp (30 mL) mayonnaise

Preheat broiler. Heat first amount of olive oil in small frying pan on medium. Add next 7 ingredients. Cook for about 1 minute, stirring often, until garlic is fragrant. Remove from heat. Add bread crumbs and Parmesan cheese. Stir.

Heat second amount of olive oil in large frying pan on medium-high. Sprinkle steak spice on both sides of steak. Add to frying pan. Cook for about 3 minutes per side until browned (see Tip).

Meanwhile, combine mustard and mayonnaise in small cup. Spread over steak. Press bread crumb mixture over top. Broil on centre rack in oven for about 4 minutes until crust is browned and internal temperature reaches 145°F (63°C) for medium-rare or until steak reaches desired doneness. Transfer to plate. Let stand for 5 minutes before serving.

1 serving: 400 Calories; 23 g Total Fat (12 g Mono, 2.5 g Poly, 6 g Sat); 65 mg Cholesterol; 9 g Carbohydrate (less than 1 g Fibre, less than 1 g Sugar); 25 g Protein; 540 mg Sodium

Tip

This cooking time will produce a final steak doneness of medium-rare. If you like your steak more well-done, reduce heat and increase cooking time when frying on stovetop.

Filet Mignon with Asparagus and Smoked Salmon

Serves 4

Filet mignon is a steak cut from the centre of the tenderloin. It is wonderfully tender and uniform in size. If it's not available, any tenderloin cut is fine. This eye-catching dish will be sure to impress.

2 Tbsp (30 mL) olive oil

1/2 tsp (2 mL) no-salt seasoning

1/4 tsp (1 mL) pepper

4 beef tenderloin steaks (about 1 inch, 2.5 cm, thick) (see Tip)

1/2 lb (225 g) fresh asparagus, trimmed of tough ends

4 oz (113 g) herb-flavoured goat (chèvre) cheese, cut up

4 oz (113 g) smoked salmon, cut into thin strips

1 Tbsp (15 mL) chopped fresh chives

Combine first 3 ingredients. Brush steaks with half of olive oil mixture. Grill on direct medium-high heat for about 5 minutes per side for medium-rare or until steak reaches desired doneness. Remove to a plate; cover with foil and let stand for 10 minutes.

Toss asparagus with remaining olive oil mixture. Grill on direct medium-high heat for about 4 minutes, turning occasionally, until tender-crisp.

To serve, arrange asparagus on a serving plate. Arrange steaks over asparagus. Top with remaining 3 ingredients.

1 serving: 350 Calories; 22 g Total Fat (10 g Mono, 1.5 g Poly, 8 g Sat); 75 mg Cholesterol; 3 g Carbohydrate (1 g Fibre, 1 g Sugar); 35 g Protein; 390 mg Sodium

Tip

You may need to tie the steaks with butcher's twine to ensure a nice shape. Don't forget to remove the string before serving.

Holiday Steak

Serves 6

Perfect for a long-weekend barbecue, or some cold winter evening when you want a culinary escape to a balmy climate.

Pineapple Salsa

1 × 19 oz (540 mL) can of pineapple tidbits, drained

1 cup (250 mL) chopped red onion

1/4 cup (60 mL) chopped fresh cilantro

2 Tbsp (30 mL) lime juice

1/2 tsp (2 mL) cayenne pepper

Pineapple Marinade

2/3 cup (150 mL) steak sauce

1/2 cup (125 mL) pineapple juice

1/4 cup (60 mL) lime juice (see Tip)

1 Tbsp (15 mL) grated lime zest

1/2 tsp (2 mL) dried oregano

1/2 tsp (2 mL) ground cumin

1/4 tsp (1 mL) cayenne pepper

Steak

2 lbs (900 g) beef top sirloin (or strip loin or rib) steaks

1 clove garlic, cut in half

Pineapple Salsa: Combine all 5 ingredients in small bowl. Chill, covered, for at least 1 hour to blend flavours. Makes about 2 1/4 cups (550 mL) salsa.

Pineapple Marinade: Combine all 7 ingredients in small bowl. Stir well. Makes about 1 1/3 cups (375 mL) marinade.

Steak: Rub both sides of steaks with cut sides of garlic clove. Put steaks into large resealable plastic bag. Add marinade. Seal bag. Turn until coated. Let stand in refrigerator for 30 minutes, turning once. Remove steaks. Transfer marinade to small saucepan. Bring to a boil. Reduce heat to medium-low. Simmer, uncovered for 5 minutes. Reserve half in small bowl. Preheat gas barbecue to medium-high. Cook steaks on greased grill for 5 to 7 minutes per side, brushing often with remaining marinade, until desired doneness. Transfer to cutting board. Tent with foil. Let stand for 10 minutes. Spoon reserved marinade over steaks. Serve with salsa.

1 serving: 400 Calories; 14 g Total Fat (6 g Mono, 0.5 g Poly, 5 g Sat); 75 mg Cholesterol; 23 g Carbohydrate (2 g Fibre, 15 g Sugar); 30 g Protein; 470 mg Sodium

Tip

When a recipe calls for grated zest and juice, it's easier
to grate the zest first, then juice the fruit. Be careful not to
grate down to the pith, which is bitter and best avoided.

Garlic Herb-crusted Steaks

Serves 4

Delicious steaks with a crisp, seasoned topping and tasty Dijon flavour. This special steak dinner is ideal for winter days because it requires the oven.

2 tsp (10 mL) cooking oil

1 lb (454 g) beef rib-eye steak, cut into 4 equal portions

salt, sprinkle

1/2 tsp (2 mL) pepper

3/4 cup (175 mL) fresh bread crumbs

2 Tbsp (30 mL) grated onion

1 tsp (5 mL) chopped fresh rosemary

1 tsp (5 mL) chopped fresh thyme

2 cloves garlic, minced

4 tsp (20 mL) butter, melted

4 tsp (20 mL) Dijon mustard

Heat cooking oil in large frying pan on medium-high. Sprinkle both sides of steaks with salt and pepper. Add to frying pan. Cook for about 2 minutes per side until browned. Transfer to greased wire rack set in large baking sheet with sides. Let stand for 5 minutes.

Combine next 5 ingredients in small bowl. Drizzle with butter. Toss.

Brush tops of steaks with mustard. Press bread crumb mixture onto mustard. Cook on centre rack in 400°F (200°C) oven for about 15 minutes until internal temperature reaches 160°F (70°C) for medium or until steaks reach desired doneness. Cover loosely with foil. Let stand for 10 minutes before serving.

1 serving: 390 Calories; 24 g Total Fat (11 g Mono, 1.5 g Poly, 10 g Sat); 90 mg Cholesterol; 19 g Carbohydrate (less than 1 g Fibre, less than 1 g Sugar); 26 g Protein; 410 mg Sodium

Rolled Steak Florentine

Serves 8

An inexpensive company dish. Serve with rice and asparagus for a truly wonderful meal.

2 1/4 lbs (1 kg) flank (or round) steak

10 oz (285 g) fresh (or frozen) spinach, cooked, squeezed dry and chopped

1 cup (250 mL) fresh bread crumbs

1 cup (250 mL) grated medium Cheddar cheese

1 large egg, fork-beaten

1/2 tsp (2 mL) poultry seasoning

1/4 tsp (1 mL) no-salt seasoning

pepper, to taste

1 × 7 1/2 oz (213 mL) can of tomato sauce

1/2 cup (125 mL) boiling water

1 tsp (5 mL) beef bouillon powder

1 clove garlic, minced

1/4 cup (60 mL) cold water

1 Tbsp (15 mL) cornstarch

Cut steak into eight 3 × 4 inch (7.5 × 10 cm) pieces. Pound with mallet or rolling pin to 1/4 inch (6 mm) thickness.

Combine next 7 ingredients in large bowl. Mix well. Divide and spread evenly over surface of each steak. Roll up, jelly roll-style, starting with narrow edge. Tie with butcher's string or secure with metal skewers. Broil rolls 4 inches (10 cm) from heat, turning until nicely browned on all sides. Place in ungreased 3 quart (3 L) casserole.

Combine tomato sauce, boiling water, bouillon powder and garlic in small bowl. Pour over rolls. Cover. Bake in 350°F (175°C) oven for 1 1/2 hours, turning rolls after 1 hour, until tender. Remove rolls to warm platter. Pour juices into small saucepan.

Stir cold water into cornstarch in small cup until smooth. Slowly stir into juices. Heat and stir until thickened. Drizzle on steak rolls. Serve.

1 serving: 350 Calories;
15 g Total Fat (5 g Mono,
0.5 g Poly, 7 g Sat);
95 mg Cholesterol;
16 g Carbohydrate
(2 g Fibre, 2 g Sugar);
35 g Protein;
640 mg Sodium

Sweet and Sour Meatballs

Serves 4

Preparing your own sweet and sour sauce results in lower fat and fewer calories than using store-bought sauce. Serve with rice.

1 cup (250 mL) cooked long-grain brown rice (about 1/4 cup, 60 mL, uncooked)

1/4 cup (60 mL) diced canned water chestnuts

1/4 cup (60 mL) grated onion

1/4 tsp (1 mL) salt

1/2 tsp (2 mL) pepper

3/4 lb (340 g) lean ground beef

1 × 14 oz (398 mL) can of crushed pineapple (with juice)

1/4 cup (60 mL) apricot jam

2 Tbsp (30 mL) rice vinegar

2 Tbsp (30 mL) soy sauce

1 Tbsp (15 mL) cornstarch

2 tsp (10 mL) grated ginger root

Combine first 5 ingredients in large bowl. Add beef. Mix well. Shape into 1 inch (2.5 cm) balls. Arrange in single layer on greased baking sheet. Cook in 400°F (200°C) oven for about 15 minutes until no longer pink inside. Makes about 30 meatballs.

Combine remaining 6 ingredients in large saucepan. Bring to a boil. Reduce heat to medium-low. Boil gently, uncovered, for about 5 minutes, stirring often, until thickened. Add meatballs. Stir gently until coated. Serve.

1 serving: 370 Calories; 12 g Total Fat (5 g Mono, 0 g Poly, 4.5 g Sat); 50 mg Cholesterol; 41 g Carbohydrate (2 g Fibre, 27 g Sugar); 19 g Protein; 530 mg Sodium

Saucy Stovetop Patties

Serves 4

For a change, serve up hamburgers Salisbury steak-style! With rich mushroom gravy, this homey dish is sure to satisfy.

1 large egg, fork-beaten

1/2 cup (125 mL) fine dry bread crumbs (see Tip, page 86)

1/4 cup (60 mL) diced onion

1 tsp (5 mL) Montreal steak spice

1 lb (454 g) lean ground beef

2 tsp (10 mL) cooking oil

1 cup (250 mL) sliced fresh white mushrooms

1 cup (250 mL) prepared beef broth

1 Tbsp (15 mL) all-purpose flour

Combine first 4 ingredients in large bowl. Add beef. Mix well. Divide into 4 equal portions. Shape into 1/2 inch (12 mm) thick patties.

Heat cooking oil in large frying pan on medium-high. Add patties. Cook for about 3 minutes per side until browned. Transfer to plate. Cover to keep warm. Reduce heat to medium.

Add mushrooms to same frying pan. Cook for about 4 minutes, stirring occasionally, until browned.

Stir broth into flour in small bowl until smooth. Slowly add to mushrooms, stirring constantly until boiling and thickened. Reduce heat to medium-low. Add patties. Turn until coated. Simmer, covered, for about 5 minutes until beef is no longer pink inside.

1 serving: 380 Calories; 20 g Total Fat (9 g Mono, 1 g Poly, 7 g Sat); 120 mg Cholesterol; 15 g Carbohydrate (less than 1 g Fibre, 2 g Sugar); 27 g Protein; 670 mg Sodium

Wheat and Wild Rice Meatloaf

Serves 8

Is your usual meatloaf a little tame? Add wild rice and some exotic Asian flavours and your meatloaf will have everyone's stomach growling.

2 tsp (10 mL) canola oil

1 cup (250 mL) diced onion

1/2 cup (125 mL) diced celery

1/2 cup (125 mL) diced red pepper

1/2 cup (125 mL) grated carrot

2 cloves garlic, minced

1 cup (250 mL) cooked hard red wheat

1 cup (250 mL) cooked wild rice

2 large eggs

1/3 cup (75 mL) balsamic vinegar

1/3 cup (75 mL) orange juice

2 Tbsp (30 mL) maple syrup

2 Tbsp (30 mL) low-sodium soy sauce

2 tsp (10 mL) chili paste (sambal oelek)

2 tsp (10 mL) sesame oil

1 1/2 lbs (680 g) extra-lean ground beef

1/2 lb (225 g) lean ground pork

Heat canola oil in large frying pan on medium. Add onion. Cook for about 5 minutes, stirring often, until starting to soften. Add next 4 ingredients. Cook for about 5 minutes, stirring occasionally, until carrot is tender-crisp. Transfer to medium bowl.

Add wheat and wild rice. Stir well.

Whisk next 7 ingredients in large bowl. Add beef and pork. Mix well. Add wheat mixture. Press into greased 9 × 5 × 3 inch (23 × 12.5 × 7.5 cm) loaf pan. Bake, uncovered, in 375°F (190°C) oven for about 80 minutes until fully cooked and internal temperature reaches 160°F (70°C). Let stand for 10 minutes. Cut into 8 slices.

1 serving: 360 Calories; 16 g Total Fat (7 g Mono, 2 g Poly, 6 g Sat); 112 mg Cholesterol; 24 g Carbohydrate (3 g Fibre, 6 g Sugar); 28 g Protein; 280 mg Sodium

Pesto Meatloaf Roll

Serves 8

Meatloaf with a mild pesto flavour. Serve with your favourite salsa for the perfect taste sensation.

1 1/2 lbs (680 g) extra-lean ground beef

1 cup (250 mL) fine dry bread crumbs (see Tip, page 86)

1 large egg

1 medium onion, diced

2 tsp (10 mL) beef bouillon powder

1/2 cup (125 mL) chopped sun-dried tomatoes, softened in boiling water for 10 minutes before chopping

3 Tbsp (45 mL) tomato paste (see Tip, page 38)

1/4 cup (60 mL) water

Pesto

1 1/2 cups (375 mL) fresh sweet basil, lightly packed

6 Tbsp (90 mL) pine nuts

3 cloves garlic, minced

6 Tbsp (90 mL) olive oil

6 Tbsp (90 mL) grated Parmesan cheese

Combine first 8 ingredients in large bowl. Mix well. Shape into 10 × 12 inch (25 × 30 cm) rectangle on greased foil.

Pesto: Measure all 5 ingredients into food processor. Process for 1 to 2 minutes until almost smooth. Spread pesto on beef mixture. Roll up, jelly roll-style, starting from long edge, using foil as a guide and pulling foil back as you roll. Carefully place roll, seam side down, on ungreased baking sheet. Bake in 325°F (160°C) oven for 1 hour. Cut into 8 slices.

1 serving: 370 Calories; 24 g Total Fat (12 g Mono, 4 g Poly, 6 g Sat); 75 mg Cholesterol; 16 g Carbohydrate (3 g Fibre, 3 g Sugar); 23 g Protein; 520 mg Sodium

Company Chili

Serves 8

A traditional full-bodied chili with a bit of zip. A good make-ahead meal. Freezes well.

2 1/2 lbs (1.1 kg) chuck steak (or stewing beef), trimmed of all visible fat, sinew removed and beef cut into 3/4 inch (2 cm) cubes

1 tsp (5 mL) cooking oil

1 large onion, chopped

3 celery ribs, chopped

1 large green pepper, chopped

2 cloves garlic, minced

2 jalapeño peppers, seeded and diced (see Tip, page 108)

1 × 28 oz (796 mL) can of diced tomatoes, with juice

1 × 5 1/2 oz (156 mL) can of tomato paste

1 cup (250 mL) water

1 1/2 Tbsp (25 mL) chili powder

1 Tbsp (15 mL) brown sugar

1 tsp (5 mL) no-salt seasoning

1/8 tsp (0.5 mL) pepper

(see next page)

Sear beef cubes in cooking oil in ovenproof Dutch oven on medium-high until browned on all sides. Reduce heat to medium.

Add next 5 ingredients. Stir. Cook for 10 minutes until vegetables are soft.

Add next 10 ingredients. Mix well. Bring to a simmer. Cover. Bake in 325°F (160°C) oven for 1 hour until beef is tender. Remove lid. Bake for 30 minutes.

Garnish individual servings with cheese and onion.

1 serving: 360 Calories; 11 g Total Fat (4 g Mono, 0.5 g Poly, 3.5 g Sat); 70 mg Cholesterol; 27 g Carbohydrate (11 g Fibre, 10 g Sugar); 38 g Protein; 630 mg Sodium

1 tsp (5 mL) Worcestershire sauce

1 Tbsp (15 mL) white vinegar

2 × 14 oz (398 mL) cans of kidney beans, drained and rinsed

grated medium Cheddar cheese, for garnish

diced red onion, for garnish

Beef and Eggplant Stew

Serves 4

Deep colour and rich flavour make this stew a real winner for dinner! Serve with buns or ciabatta bread.

2 tsp (10 mL) olive oil	Heat first amount of olive oil in large pot or Dutch oven on medium-high. Add beef. Cook for 10 to 15 minutes, stirring occasionally, until browned. Transfer to large bowl. Cover to keep warm.
1 lb (454 g) stewing beef	

2 tsp (10 mL) olive oil

4 cups (1 L) cubed eggplant

1 1/2 cups (375 mL) chopped onion

Add second amount of olive oil to same large pot. Reduce heat to medium. Add eggplant and onion. Cook for 5 to 10 minutes, stirring often, until onion is softened.

1 × 14 oz (398 mL) can of diced tomatoes, no salt added (with juice)

3/4 cup (175 mL) dry red wine

1/4 cup (60 mL) tomato paste (see Tip)

Add next 3 ingredients. Stir. Bring to a boil. Add beef. Stir. Reduce heat to medium-low. Cover. Simmer for about 1 1/2 hours, stirring occasionally, until beef is very tender. Remove cover. Bring to a boil on medium. Boil gently for about 10 minutes, stirring occasionally, until sauce is thickened.

1 × 14 oz (398 mL) can of artichoke hearts, drained and quartered

1/4 cup (60 mL) kalamata olives

2 Tbsp (30 mL) chopped fresh mint leaves

Add remaining 3 ingredients. Stir. Cook for 3 to 5 minutes, stirring occasionally, until heated through.

1 serving: 400 Calories; 17 g Total Fat (10 g Mono, 1 g Poly, 4.5 g Sat); 65 mg Cholesterol; 24 g Carbohydrate (9 g Fibre, 10 g Sugar); 29 g Protein; 730 mg Sodium

Tip

If a recipe calls for less than an entire can of tomato paste, freeze the unopened can for 30 minutes. Open both ends and push the contents through one end. Slice off only what you need. Freeze the remaining paste in a resealable freezer bag or plastic wrap for future use.

excellent!

Uptown Asparagus Chicken

Serves 4

The delightful presentation and the combination of havarti, asparagus and ham over lemon-peppered chicken is well worth the preparation.

1 lb (454 g) fresh asparagus, trimmed of tough ends

4 boneless, skinless chicken breast halves (4–6 oz, 113–170 g, each)

2 Tbsp (30 mL) cooking oil

3 Tbsp (45 mL) balsamic vinegar

1/2 tsp (2 mL) lemon pepper

4 thin deli ham slices (about 4 oz, 113 g)

3/4 cup (175 mL) roasted red peppers, drained and blotted dry, cut into strips

4 slices of havarti cheese, cut diagonally into triangles (about 4 oz, 113 g)

Blanch asparagus in boiling salted water in medium frying pan for about 2 minutes until bright green. Drain. Immediately plunge into ice water in large bowl. Let stand for 5 minutes. Drain well.

Place 1 chicken breast between 2 sheets of plastic wrap. Pound with mallet or rolling pin to 1/2 inch (12 mm) thickness. Transfer to greased baking sheet with sides. Repeat with remaining chicken. Mix cooking oil and balsamic vinegar together and then brush onto chicken. Sprinkle with lemon pepper. Broil on top rack in oven for about 7 minutes until golden brown and internal temperature reaches 170°F (75°C).

Place 1 slice of ham, folding if necessary, on each chicken breast. Place 3 or 4 asparagus spears over ham. Arrange red pepper strips over asparagus. Overlap 2 triangles of cheese over red pepper. Broil for about 2 minutes until cheese is melted and bubbling.

1 serving: 350 Calories; 17 g Total Fat (3.5 g Mono, 2 g Poly, 7 g Sat); 105 mg Cholesterol; 9 g Carbohydrate (3 g Fibre, 5 g Sugar); 41 g Protein; 640 mg Sodium

Chicken Papreeks

Serves 2

Tender, cherry-smoked chicken with a vibrant seasoning of fresh lemon, oregano and mighty paprika. Also makes a great low-calorie barbecue recipe without smoking.

2 cups (500 mL) cherry wood chips with smoke box (optional)

water, to cover

1/2 cup (125 mL) lemon juice

1 Tbsp (15 mL) canola oil

1 tsp (5 mL) white balsamic vinegar

1/2 tsp (2 mL) grainy mustard

1 tsp (5 mL) paprika

1/2 tsp (2 mL) chopped fresh oregano

1/4 tsp (1 mL) salt

1/4 tsp (1 mL) pepper

2 bone-in chicken thighs (5–6 oz, 140–170 g, each), skin removed

2 chicken drumsticks (3–5 oz, 85–140 g, each), skin removed

Place cherry wood chips in large bowl. Add enough water to completely cover, and let soak for at least 30 minutes.

Mix together next 8 ingredients in small bowl. Pour marinade into resealable plastic bag. Add chicken. Shake well, then remove excess air from bag and allow to sit for at least 20 minutes.

Preheat barbecue to medium. Preheat smoke box on grill. Place soaked cherry chips in smoke box. Once wood chips begin smoking, about 15 to 20 minutes, add chicken to grill. Close lid. Grill for about 10 minutes, turning occasionally. Reduce heat to low and move chicken to edges of grill. Close lid and cook for an additional 4 minutes. Without opening lid, turn barbecue off and allow chicken to rest on grill for 5 minutes (see Tip). Serve.

1 serving: 370 Calories; 17 g Total Fat (6 g Mono, 3 g Poly, 2 g Sat); 180 mg Cholesterol; 7 g Carbohydrate (less than 1 g Fibre, 2 g Sugar); 47 g Protein; 420 mg Sodium

Tip

It is important to keep the lid of the barbecue closed as much as possible to absorb the most flavour from the cherry wood chips.

Greek Chicken Thighs

Serves 4

Easy and delicious, the Mediterranean ingredients for this dish offer full-bodied colour and flavour. Hide your best china—guests may want to smash plates in approval as the Greeks used to do.

1 1/2 large red peppers

1 1/2 large yellow peppers

2 Tbsp (30 mL) Greek dressing

1/4 cup (60 mL) black olive tapenade

1/4 cup (60 mL) dry white wine

1/4 cup (60 mL) Greek yogurt

2 cloves garlic, minced

8 boneless, skinless chicken thighs (about 3 oz, 85 g, each)

1 large lemon, halved

1/2 cup (125 mL) crumbled feta cheese

1 Tbsp (15 mL) fresh oregano leaves

Grill red and yellow peppers, skin-side down, on direct medium-high heat for about 10 minutes until skins are blistered and blackened. Remove to plate. Tent with foil. Let stand until cool enough to handle. Remove and discard skins. Cut peppers into long strips. Toss with dressing and set aside.

Combine tapenade, wine, yogurt and garlic in a large resealable plastic bag. Add chicken and chill for 30 minutes. Drain and discard marinade. Grill chicken on direct medium heat for about 7 minutes per side until internal temperature reaches 170°F (75°C).

Squeeze lemon over chicken. Sprinkle with feta cheese and oregano. Serve with grilled peppers.

1 serving: 350 Calories; 19 g Total Fat (6 g Mono, 2 g Poly, 6 g Sat); 115 mg Cholesterol; 21 g Carbohydrate (3 g Fibre, 5 g Sugar); 27 g Protein; 460 mg Sodium

Curry Yogurt Chicken with Tomato Mango Salsa

Serves 4

The best thing about curry is layer upon layer of flavour, and this recipe is a perfect example. Easy and delicious.

1/4 cup (60 mL) mild curry paste

1/4 cup (60 mL) tomato paste (see Tip, page 38)

1/2 cup (125 mL) beer

3/4 cup (175 mL) Greek yogurt

4 boneless, skinless chicken breast halves (4–6 oz, 113–170 g, each)

Tomato Mango Salsa

1 1/2 cups (375 mL) diced seeded tomato

1 1/2 cups (375 mL) diced fresh mango

1/2 cup (125 mL) diced peeled kiwi fruit

1/2 cup (125 mL) diced red onion

1 Tbsp (15 mL) chopped fresh cilantro

3 Tbsp (45 mL) dry white wine

1 Tbsp (15 mL) lime juice

2 tsp (10 mL) olive oil

1 clove garlic, crushed

1/4 tsp (1 mL) no-salt seasoning

Preheat grill to medium. Combine first 4 ingredients in large bowl. Add chicken. Turn to coat chicken. Grill chicken for 4 to 6 minutes per side until tender and cooked through. Brush with extra yogurt mixture as needed.

Tomato Mango Salsa: Combine all 10 ingredients in medium bowl. Makes 4 cups (1 L) salsa. Serve with chicken.

1 serving: 350 Calories; 9 g Total Fat (2 g Mono, 1 g Poly, 3.5 g Sat); 75 mg Cholesterol; 32 g Carbohydrate (4 g Fibre, 19 g Sugar); 31 g Protein; 740 mg Sodium

Mango-stuffed Chicken

Serves 6

The tropical taste comes alive on the barbecue!

1 cup (250 mL) diced ripe mango

1/2 cup (125 mL) chopped salted macadamia nuts

3 Tbsp (45 mL) flaked coconut

3 Tbsp (45 mL) thinly sliced green onion

1/2 tsp (2 mL) grated lime zest

1/2 tsp (2 mL) curry powder

6 boneless, skinless chicken breast halves (4–6 oz, 113–170 g, each)

6 toothpicks, soaked in water

Lime Yogurt Marinade

1 1/2 cups (375 mL) plain yogurt

1/4 cup (60 mL) lime juice

1 Tbsp (15 mL) ground coriander

1 Tbsp (15 mL) curry powder

2 tsp (10 mL) grated ginger root

4 cloves garlic, minced

1 tsp (5 mL) no-salt seasoning

Combine first 6 ingredients in medium bowl. Stir.

Cut deep pocket into side of each chicken breast almost through to other side. Spoon mango mixture into each pocket. Secure with toothpick. Place stuffed chicken breasts in large shallow baking dish.

Lime Yogurt Marinade: Combine all 7 ingredients in small bowl. Makes about 1 3/4 cups (425 mL) marinade. Pour over chicken. Turn until coated. Cover with plastic wrap. Marinate in refrigerator for at least 3 hours, turning occasionally. Drain and discard marinade.

Preheat barbecue to medium. Place chicken breasts on 1 side of greased grill over drip pan. Turn off burner under chicken, leaving opposite burner on medium. Close lid. Cook for 7 to 8 minutes. Turn chicken over. Close lid. Cook for 5 to 6 minutes until meat thermometer inserted into breast (not stuffing) reads 185°F (85°C). Remove from heat. Tent with foil. Let stand for 15 minutes before serving.

1 serving: 350 Calories; 13 g Total Fat (7 g Mono, 0.5 g Poly, 3.5 g Sat); 105 mg Cholesterol; 15 g Carbohydrate (3 g Fibre, 10 g Sugar); 45 g Protein; 140 mg Sodium

Phyllo-wrapped Chicken with Port Wine Sauce

Serves 4

Stuffed chicken breasts wrapped in phyllo and topped with a beautiful sauce—the layers of this dish add up to perfection.

1 tsp (5 mL) cooking oil

1 cup (250 mL) thinly sliced leek (white part only)

2 cloves garlic, minced

Heat cooking oil in medium non-stick frying pan on medium-low. Add leek and garlic. Cook for about 10 minutes, stirring occasionally, until leek is softened.

1 tsp (5 mL) grated orange zest

1/4 tsp (1 mL) pepper

Add orange zest and pepper. Stir. Makes about 3/4 cup (175 mL) filling.

4 boneless, skinless chicken breast halves (4–6 oz, 113–170 g, each)

Cut deep pocket into side of each chicken breast almost through to other side. Fill each pocket with 1/4 of filling. Press to seal openings.

8 frozen phyllo pastry sheets, thawed according to package directions

Lay 1 pastry sheet on waxed paper or parchment paper on counter. Cover remaining pastry with slightly damp tea towel. Lightly spray pastry sheet with cooking spray. Working quickly, lay second pastry sheet on top. Spray with cooking spray. Repeat with 2 more pastry sheets and cooking spray. Cut pastry in half crosswise. Place 1 stuffed chicken breast 1 inch (2.5 cm) from short end. Fold in each long side, slightly overlapping chicken. Roll up to enclose chicken. Place, seam-side down, on lightly greased baking sheet with sides. Repeat with remaining pastry and chicken. Lightly spray chicken parcels with cooking spray. Bake in 400°F (200°C) oven for about 15 minutes until pastry is browned.

Port Wine Sauce

1 Tbsp (15 mL) prepared chicken broth

1/2 cup (125 mL) diced onion

Port Wine Sauce: Heat first amount of broth in medium frying pan on medium. Add onion. Cook for 5 minutes until onion is softened.

1/2 cup (125 mL) port

1/2 cup (125 mL) prepared chicken broth

3 Tbsp (45 mL) redcurrant jelly

Add remaining 3 ingredients. Heat and stir until jelly melts. Bring to a boil on medium-high. Boil, uncovered, for about 10 minutes until thickened. Makes 2/3 cup (150 mL). Serve with chicken parcels.

1 serving: 400 Calories; 3.5 g Total Fat (1 g Mono, 0.5 g Poly, 1.5 g Sat); 65 mg Cholesterol; 48 g Carbohydrate (3 g Fibre, 14 g Sugar); 34 g Protein; 420 mg Sodium

Italian Colours

Serves 6

A pretty presentation of Chicken Parmigiana. Tender chicken topped with creamy white cheese, a splash of red tomato and green basil. All the colours of the Italian flag!

1/3 cup (75 mL) all-purpose flour

1 tsp (5 mL) no-salt seasoning, herb and garlic blend

pepper, sprinkle

1 large egg

2 Tbsp (30 mL) olive oil

1 Tbsp (15 mL) milk

2/3 cup (150 mL) fine dry bread crumbs (see Tip, page 86)

1/4 cup (60 mL) chopped fresh parsley

3 Tbsp (45 mL) grated Parmesan cheese

6 boneless, skinless chicken breast halves (4–6 oz, 113–170 g, each)

6 tomato slices

6 provolone (or mozzarella) cheese slices (about 4 oz, 113 g)

2 Tbsp (30 mL) chopped fresh basil

Mix first 3 ingredients in shallow dish.

Beat next 3 ingredients in small bowl with fork.

Mix next 3 ingredients in separate shallow dish.

Dredge chicken in flour mixture. Dip into egg mixture. Coat well in crumb mixture. Arrange on greased baking sheet. Bake, uncovered, in 375°F (190°C) oven for about 25 minutes until golden brown and no longer pink inside.

Place 1 slice of tomato, 1 slice of provolone cheese and a sprinkle of basil on top of each chicken breast. Heat in oven for about 5 minutes until cheese is melted.

1 serving: 370 Calories; 13 g Total Fat (5 g Mono, 1.5 g Poly, 6 g Sat); 115 mg Cholesterol; 16 g Carbohydrate (1 g Fibre, 2 g Sugar); 38 g Protein; 470 mg Sodium

Elegant Chicken Phyllo

Serves 1

Multiply this recipe by the number of servings you'll need. If you prepare it in the morning, brush the phyllo with melted butter and cover with plastic wrap before refrigerating.

2 phyllo pastry sheets, thawed according to package directions

1 Tbsp (15 mL) butter, melted

1 Tbsp (15 mL) light spreadable cream cheese, mashed with fork

1 1/2 tsp (7 mL) chopped pimiento

1 boneless, skinless chicken breast half (4–6 oz, 113–170 g), pounded flat and cut into thin strips

salt, sprinkle

pepper, sprinkle

1 medium fresh white mushroom, sliced

Lay 1 sheet of pastry on working surface. Brush sheet with melted butter. Fold in half crosswise. Repeat with second pastry sheet. Place second sheet crosswise over first sheet.

Spread cream cheese in 4 inch (10 cm) diameter circle in centre of pastry. Layer next 5 ingredients in order given, over top. Gather ends of pastry sheets and press together at top of filling to enclose, allowing corners to flare outward. Place on greased baking sheet. Bake in 350°F (175°C) oven for about 30 minutes until pastry is browned and crisp. Serve immediately.

1 serving: 400 Calories; 18 g Total Fat (3.5 g Mono, 1 g Poly, 10 g Sat); 115 mg Cholesterol; 24 g Carbohydrate (2 g Fibre, 3 g Sugar); 34 g Protein; 440 mg Sodium

Spiff Duck

Serves 2

Tropical fruit and fresh rosemary make this crispy duck burst with flavour. Search for naturally raised duck.

1 Tbsp (15 mL) olive oil

1 tsp (5 mL) white balsamic vinegar

1/4 tsp (1 mL) chopped fresh rosemary

1/4 tsp (1 mL) salt

1/4 tsp (1 mL) pepper

1/8 tsp (0.5 mL) ground cloves

2 duck breasts (about 6 oz, 170 g, each), fat trimmed

1/3 cup (75 mL) water

2 Tbsp (30 mL) orange juice

1 passion fruit, chopped

1/2 cup (125 mL) sugar pea shoots

2 Tbsp (30 mL) crushed cashews

Combine first 6 ingredients in medium bowl; mix well. Add duck breasts and turn to coat. Cover with plastic wrap. Allow to marinate at room temperature for at least 30 minutes.

Heat medium cast iron or other oven-proof pan over medium-high. Add duck breasts, fat side down. Cook for 6 to 8 minutes, without flipping, to render fat. Pour off and discard melted fat as it accumulates. Watch closely to avoid burning; adjust heat if necessary. Transfer duck to plate. Tent with foil. Set aside.

Return pan to stove over high. Once pan just begins to lightly smoke, pour in water and stir aggressively with rubber spatula. When water has reached a boil, add orange juice. Cook until reduced by half. Reduce heat to low. Add passion fruit and cook for 2 to 3 minutes, until liquid is the consistency of thin syrup. Return duck to pan, cooked side up. Place entire pan in 400°F (200°C) oven. Cook for 4 to 5 minutes for medium doneness. Cook for an additional 3 minutes for well done. Remove from oven. Let stand for 5 to 8 minutes.

To serve, place a spoonful of sauce on a plate, then duck breast. Spoon more sauce over duck and top with pea shoots. Dust with cashews.

1 serving: 370 Calories; 19 g Total Fat (5 g Mono, 2 g Poly, 5 g Sat); 135 mg Cholesterol; 12 g Carbohydrate (2 g Fibre, 3 g Sugar); 37 g Protein; 390 mg Sodium

Thai Turkey Steaks

Serves 4

Both sweet and spicy, as well as creamy and crunchy, this dish offers gorgeous visual elements with a colourful carrot, cucumber and mango topping.

1 Tbsp (15 mL) lime juice

1 tsp (5 mL) sugar

1/2 cup (125 mL) julienned carrot

1/2 cup (125 mL) julienned English cucumber

1/2 cup (125 mL) julienned fresh mango

2 boneless, skinless turkey breast steaks (about 1 inch, 2.5 cm, thick), cut in halft

1 Tbsp (15 mL) olive oil

salt, sprinkle

pepper, sprinkle

1 cup (250 mL) coconut milk

1 tsp (5 mL) Thai green curry paste

3/4 tsp (4 mL) sugar

1/4 tsp (1 mL) salt

1 Tbsp (15 mL) lime juice

1 tsp (5 mL) cornstarch

(see next page)

Stir first amount of lime juice and sugar together in a bowl until sugar is dissolved. Add next 3 ingredients and toss until coated. Chill.

Brush turkey with olive oil and sprinkle with salt and pepper. Grill on direct medium-high heat for about 4 minutes per side until internal temperature reaches 170°F (75°C). Rotate meat after 2 minutes of cooking to create attractive grill marks. Remove to a plate. Tent with foil. Let stand for 5 minutes.

Combine next 4 ingredients in a saucepan. Bring to a boil, stirring occasionally.

Stir second amount of lime juice into cornstarch. Stir into curry mixture. Heat and stir until boiling and thickened. Remove from heat.

Stir in 2 Tbsp (30 mL) of basil and 2 Tbsp (30 mL) of cilantro. Spoon onto 4 serving plates, placing steaks over sauce. Stir carrot mixture and spoon over steaks. Sprinkle with remaining basil, cilantro, peanuts and coconut.

1 serving: 360 Calories; 22 g Total Fat (5 g Mono, 2 g Poly, 13 g Sat); 60 mg Cholesterol; 14 g Carbohydrate (2 g Fibre, 7 g Sugar); 28 g Protein; 350 mg Sodium

〰 *If turkey steaks are not available at your local supermarket, you can buy boneless, skinless turkey breast and cut it into half-inch-thick slices yourself. It is easier to do if the turkey is slightly frozen.*

1/4 cup (60 mL) chopped
fresh basil

1/4 cup (60 mL) chopped
fresh cilantro

1/4 cup (60 mL) coarsely
chopped salted peanuts

2 Tbsp (30 mL) flaked
coconut

Ginger Pineapple Meatballs

Serves 4

These tangy meatballs are not too sweet, not too sour and not too spicy. Serve over rice.

1 large egg, fork-beaten

1/2 cup (125 mL) fine dry bread crumbs (see Tip, page 86)

1/4 cup (60 mL) diced red pepper

1/4 cup (60 mL) grated onion

1/2 tsp (2 mL) ground ginger

1/2 tsp (2 mL) no-salt seasoning

1/4 tsp (1 mL) pepper

1 lb (454 g) lean ground turkey

2 tsp (10 mL) cooking oil

1 × 14 oz (398 mL) can of crushed pineapple (with juice)

1/2 cup (125 mL) sweet chili sauce

1 Tbsp (15 mL) lime juice

2 tsp (10 mL) grated ginger root

1/4 tsp (1 mL) salt

1 Tbsp (15 mL) low-sodium soy sauce

2 tsp (10 mL) cornstarch

1/4 cup (60 mL) sliced green onion

Combine first 7 ingredients in medium bowl. Add turkey. Mix well. Roll into 1 inch (2.5 cm) balls. Heat cooking oil in large frying pan on medium-high. Add meatballs. Cook for 5 to 10 minutes, turning often, until fully cooked and internal temperature reaches 175°F (80°C). Transfer with slotted spoon to plate lined with paper towel to drain.

Add next 5 ingredients to same frying pan.

Stir soy sauce into cornstarch in small cup. Add to pineapple mixture. Heat and stir until boiling and thickened. Add meatballs. Stir until coated. Reduce heat to medium-low. Cook for about 5 minutes until heated through. Sprinkle with green onion before serving.

1 serving: 350 Calories; 6 g Total Fat (2 g Mono, 1 g Poly, 1 g Sat); 115 mg Cholesterol; 44 g Carbohydrate (2 g Fibre, 28 g Sugar); 30 g Protein; 530 mg Sodium

Anise Chicken

Serves 4

Toss steamed snow peas with toasted sesame seeds and add some jasmine rice to the menu for an Asian-inspired meal.

1 Tbsp (15 mL) cooking oil

4 boneless, skinless chicken breast halves (4–6 oz, 113–170 g, each), cut in half

2 cloves garlic, minced

1 Tbsp (15 mL) grated ginger root

1 Tbsp (15 mL) Chinese cooking wine

1/4 cup (60 mL) prepared low-sodium chicken broth

1/4 cup (60 mL) liquid honey

3 Tbsp (45 mL) low-sodium soy sauce

1 star anise

1/2 tsp (2 mL) pepper

1 Tbsp (15 mL) water

1 1/2 tsp (7 mL) cornstarch

sliced green onion, for garnish

Heat cooking oil in wok or large frying pan on medium-high. Cook chicken, in 2 batches, for 3 minutes per side until lightly browned. Remove from wok.

Add garlic and ginger to same wok. Cook for about 1 minute until fragrant.

Add next 6 ingredients. Bring to a boil on high. Reduce heat to medium-high. Add chicken. Cover. Simmer for 10 to 15 minutes until chicken is no longer pink inside. Remove and discard star anise.

Stir water into cornstarch in small bowl until smooth. Stir into chicken mixture. Heat and stir for 1 to 2 minutes until sauce is boiling and thickened. Garnish with green onion.

1 serving: 350 Calories; 6 g Total Fat (2.5 g Mono, 1.5 g Poly, 1 g Sat); 115 mg Cholesterol; 26 g Carbohydrate (0 g Fibre, 22 g Sugar); 47 g Protein; 620 mg Sodium

Star anise is a star-shaped spice with a mild licorice flavour. Look for it in grocery, spice and specialty food stores.

Fragrant Chicken and Rice

Serves 8

Now, this is what we call aromatherapy! As this wholesome, zesty rice dish simmers, revel in the soothing and delicious fragrance that will draw everyone to the kitchen.

1 Tbsp (15 mL) cooking oil

1 lb (454 g) boneless, skinless chicken thighs, cut into 1 inch (2.5 cm) pieces

2 cups (500 mL) chopped onion

1/2 tsp (2 mL) ground cinnamon

1/2 tsp (2 mL) ground coriander

1/2 tsp (2 mL) ground cumin

1/4 tsp (1 mL) garlic powder

1/4 tsp (1 mL) pepper

2 1/2 cups (625 mL) prepared chicken broth

1 × 19 oz (540 mL) can of chickpeas (garbanzo beans), rinsed and drained

1 cup (250 mL) long-grain white rice

1/2 cup (125 mL) chopped dried apricot

1 1/2 Tbsp (22 mL) honey

1/4 tsp (1 mL) salt

(see next page)

Heat cooking oil in large frying pan on medium. Add chicken. Cook for about 5 minutes, stirring occasionally, until starting to brown. Remove to plate.

Add onion to same frying pan. Cook for 5 to 10 minutes, stirring occasionally, until softened.

Add next 5 ingredients. Heat and stir for about 1 minute until fragrant.

Add next 6 ingredients and chicken. Stir. Bring to a boil. Reduce heat to medium-low. Simmer, covered, for 30 minutes, without stirring. Remove from heat. Let stand, covered, for about 5 minutes until liquid is absorbed and rice is tender. Fluff with fork.

Add remaining 3 ingredients. Toss gently and serve.

1 serving: 350 Calories; 9 g Total Fat (4 g Mono, 2 g Poly, 1 g Sat); 45 mg Cholesterol; 47 g Carbohydrate (6 g Fibre, 10 g Sugar); 21 g Protein; 470 mg Sodium

Tip

When toasting nuts, seeds or coconut, cooking times will vary for each type of nut—so never toast them together. For small amounts, place the ingredient in an ungreased shallow frying pan. Heat on medium for 3 to 5 minutes, stirring often, until golden. For larger amounts, spread the ingredient evenly in an ungreased shallow pan. Bake in a 350°F (175°C) oven for 5 to 10 minutes, stirring or shaking often, until golden.

1/2 cup (125 mL) sliced
almonds, toasted (see Tip)

2 Tbsp (30 mL) chopped
fresh chives

1/2 tsp (2 mL) grated lemon
zest

Chicken Ratatouille

Serves 4

Send your taste buds on a trip with this robust dish that's full of bold Mediterranean flavours. It goes great with crusty bread or pasta.

1/3 cup (75 mL) all-purpose flour

1/2 tsp (2 mL) no-salt seasoning, Italian blend

1/4 tsp (1 mL) pepper

4 boneless, skinless chicken breast halves (4–6 oz, 113–170 g, each), cut in half

1 Tbsp (15 mL) cooking oil

3 cups (750 mL) diced eggplant (with peel)

1 cup (250 mL) chopped onion

1 × 14 oz (398 mL) can of diced tomatoes (with juice)

1 cup (250 mL) chopped green pepper

1 cup (250 mL) chopped red pepper

1 cup (250 mL) sliced fresh white mushrooms

(see next page)

Combine first 3 ingredients in large resealable plastic bag. Add chicken. Toss until coated. Remove chicken. Discard any remaining flour mixture.

Heat cooking oil in large frying pan on medium-high. Add chicken. Cook for about 2 minutes per side until browned. Remove to plate.

Add eggplant and onion to same frying pan. Cook for about 5 minutes, stirring often and scraping any brown bits from bottom of pan, until browned and starting to soften.

Add next 9 ingredients and chicken. Stir. Bring to a boil. Reduce heat to medium-low. Simmer, covered, for about 30 minutes until chicken is no longer pink inside and vegetables are tender.

Sprinkle with Parmesan cheese before serving.

1 serving: 350 Calories; 7 g Total Fat (3 g Mono, 1.5 g Poly, 1.5 g Sat); 100 mg Cholesterol; 26 g Carbohydrate (5 g Fibre, 12 g Sugar); 45 g Protein; 480 mg Sodium

2 tsp (10 mL) sugar

1 tsp (5 mL) dried basil

1/2 tsp (2 mL) dried thyme

1/2 tsp (2 mL) garlic powder

1/2 tsp (2 mL) no-salt seasoning, Italian blend

2 Tbsp (30 mL) grated Parmesan cheese

Spring Chicken Pot Pie

Serves 4

Using only a top crust for this hearty pot pie cuts way back on fat and calories. To make this recipe gluten-free, use gluten-free chicken broth.

2 tsp (10 mL) canola oil

3/4 lb (340 g) boneless, skinless chicken breast halves, cut into 3/4 inch (2 cm) pieces

1 1/2 cups (375 mL) sliced leek (white part only)

1 cup (250 mL) diced unpeeled potato

2 cloves garlic, minced

1/4 tsp (1 mL) no-salt seasoning

1/4 tsp (1 mL) pepper

1 1/2 cups (375 mL) prepared low-sodium chicken broth

2 Tbsp (30 mL) cornstarch

1 cup (250 mL) chopped trimmed asparagus

1 cup (250 mL) frozen peas, thawed

3 cups (750 mL) prepared low-sodium chicken broth

1 cup (250 mL) yellow cornmeal

1 Tbsp (15 mL) chopped green onion

1 Tbsp (15 mL) chopped fresh dill

Heat canola oil in large saucepan on medium. Add next 6 ingredients. Cook for about 10 minutes, stirring often, until chicken is no longer pink and potato is tender.

Stir first amount of broth into cornstarch in small bowl. Add to chicken mixture. Bring to a boil. Cook for 2 minutes, stirring occasionally.

Add asparagus and peas. Stir. Transfer to greased 8 × 8 inch (20 × 20 cm) baking dish.

Bring second amount of broth to a boil in medium saucepan. Add cornmeal. Heat and stir for about 5 minutes until mixture thickens and pulls away from side of pan. Stir in green onion and dill. Pour evenly over chicken mixture. Bake in 375°F (190°C) oven for about 35 minutes until bubbling and topping is set.

1 serving: 380 Calories; 3.5 g Total Fat (1.5 g Mono, 1 g Poly, 0.5 g Sat); 50 mg Cholesterol; 55 g Carbohydrate (5 g Fibre, 6 g Sugar); 30 g Protein; 850 mg Sodium

Arroz con Pollo

Serves 6

Literally "rice with chicken," this Latin American dish will be something your family asks for often. Saffron is a bit more expensive than other spices, but it adds a special touch.

3 1/2 lbs (1.6 kg) bone-in chicken parts, skin removed

1 1/2 cups (375 mL) boiling low-sodium prepared chicken broth

1 1/2 cups (375 mL) boiling water

2 1/2 cups (625 mL) frozen peas

1 × 14 oz (398 mL) can of diced tomatoes (with juice)

1 1/2 cups (375 mL) long-grain white rice

1 cup (250 mL) diced red pepper

1/2 cup (125 mL) diced onion

1 × 2 oz (57 mL) jar of pimiento, well drained and chopped

1/2 tsp (2 mL) dried basil

1 tsp (5 mL) no-salt seasoning, garlic and herb blend

1/4 tsp (1 mL) pepper

1/4 tsp (1 mL) saffron threads (or turmeric)

1/4 tsp (1 mL) garlic powder

Arrange chicken in greased 9 × 13 inch (23 × 33 cm) pan. Bake, uncovered, in 350°F (175°C) oven for 30 minutes. Transfer to large plate.

Combine remaining 13 ingredients in same pan. Arrange chicken on rice mixture. Cover with greased foil. Bake for another 35 to 45 minutes until chicken is no longer pink inside, rice is tender and liquid is absorbed.

1 serving: 350 Calories; 4 g Total Fat (1 g Mono, 1 g Poly, 1 g Sat); 60 mg Cholesterol; 51 g Carbohydrate (4 g Fibre, 9 g Sugar); 26 g Protein; 340 mg Sodium

Orange Spice Chicken Casserole

Serves 8

When the right fruit is paired with the right meat—as in this wonderful winter warmer—it makes for a very satisfying entree. This casserole's slightly spicy sauce has aroma and flavour appeal.

1 cup (250 mL) orange juice

1/2 cup (125 mL) dry white wine

1/4 cup (60 mL) liquid honey

2 Tbsp (30 mL) olive oil

2 tsp (10 mL) ground coriander

2 tsp (10 mL) ground cumin

2 tsp (10 mL) ground ginger

1 tsp (5 mL) chili powder

1 tsp (5 mL) pepper

1/2 tsp (2 mL) ground cinnamon

1/2 tsp (2 mL) salt

1 cup (250 mL) pitted prunes

1 cup (250 mL) dried apricots, halved

1/2 cup (125 mL) pimiento-stuffed olives

2 1/4 lbs (1 kg) boneless, skinless chicken thighs, halved

1 medium orange, cut into 1/4 inch (6 mm) slices

Combine first 11 ingredients in small bowl.

Place next 3 ingredients in 3 quart (3 L) casserole. Arrange chicken over top. Pour orange juice mixture over chicken.

Arrange orange slices over chicken. Cover. Bake in 350°F (175°C) oven for 30 minutes. Remove cover. Bake for 50 minutes, basting twice, until sauce is slightly thickened and chicken is tender.

1 serving: 350 Calories; 9 g Total Fat (4.5 g Mono, 1.5 g Poly, 2 g Sat); 105 mg Cholesterol; 38 g Carbohydrate (4 g Fibre, 25 g Sugar); 27 g Protein; 380 mg Sodium

Chicken and Bean Casserole

Serves 8

Baked slowly in a fragrant tomato broth, this nourishing casserole is ideal for a relaxed dinner with friends. Lemon and parsley add a fresh touch.

1 lb (454 g) dried navy beans (about 2 1/3 cups, 575 mL)

water, to cover

1 Tbsp (15 mL) olive oil

8 bone-in chicken thighs, skin removed

2 cups (500 mL) chopped onion

1 cup (250 mL) chopped fennel bulb (or celery)

2 cups (500 mL) prepared low-sodium chicken broth

1 cup (250 mL) dry white wine

1 × 14 oz (398 mL) can of diced tomatoes (with juice)

6 cloves garlic, minced

2 bay leaves

1 tsp (5 mL) pepper

1 medium lemon, ends removed, cut into 8 slices

1/2 cup (125 mL) chopped fresh parsley

1 tsp (5 mL) no-salt seasoning

Soak beans in water in large bowl overnight. Drain. Put into lightly greased 4 quart (4 L) casserole dish.

Heat olive oil in large frying pan on medium-high. Add chicken. Cook until browned on both sides. Remove from frying pan. Set aside.

Add onion and fennel to same frying pan. Cook for about 5 minutes until onion is softened.

Add onion mixture and next 6 ingredients to beans. Mix well. Nestle chicken into bean mixture.

Place 1 lemon slice over each chicken thigh. Cover. Bake in 350°F (175°C) oven for 3 1/2 hours until beans are softened.

Remove and discard lemon slices and bay leaves. Remove chicken. Add parsley and no-salt seasoning to beans. Stir. Serve with chicken.

1 serving: 350 Calories; 4.5 g Total Fat (2 g Mono, 1 g Poly, 1 g Sat); 50 mg Cholesterol; 48 g Carbohydrate (16 g Fibre, 12 g Sugar); 25 g Protein; 390 mg Sodium

Mediterranean Chicken

Serves 6

Treat your guests to the flavours of the Mediterranean with tender, juicy chicken covered in a rustic sauce of tomatoes, olives and oregano.

1/4 cup (60 mL) chopped fresh oregano

1/4 cup (60 mL) dry white wine

1/4 cup (60 mL) olive oil

2 Tbsp (30 mL) lemon juice

2 cloves garlic, minced

2 tsp (10 mL) grated lemon zest (see Tip, page 23)

2 tsp (10 mL) liquid honey

1/4 tsp (1 mL) salt

1/4 tsp (1 mL) pepper

6 boneless, skinless chicken breast halves (4–6 oz, 113–170 g, each)

1/3 cup (75 mL) all-purpose flour

1 Tbsp (15 mL) olive oil

1 tsp (5 mL) olive oil

1 1/2 cups (375 mL) chopped onion

(see next page)

Combine first 9 ingredients in small bowl.

Put chicken into large resealable plastic bag. Add oregano mixture. Seal bag. Turn until coated. Let stand in refrigerator for 1 to 2 hours, turning occasionally. Remove chicken. Set aside remaining oregano mixture. Pat chicken dry with paper towels.

Measure flour onto plate. Press both sides of chicken into flour. Heat second amount of olive oil in large frying pan on medium-high. Add chicken. Cook for 2 to 4 minutes per side until browned. Arrange chicken in single layer in ungreased 2 quart (2 L) casserole. Set aside. Reduce heat to medium.

Add third amount of olive oil to same frying pan. Add onion. Cook for 5 to 10 minutes, stirring occasionally, until onion is softened.

Add tomatoes and reserved oregano mixture. Bring to a boil. Reduce heat to medium-low. Simmer, uncovered, for about 5 minutes until liquid is reduced.

Add olives and cream. Stir. Pour over chicken. Bake, covered, in 350°F (175°C) oven for about 30 minutes until bubbling and chicken is tender.

To serve, arrange 2 lemon slices over each chicken breast. Sprinkle with oregano.

1 serving: 350 Calories; 17 g Total Fat (11 g Mono, 1.5 g Poly, 2.5 g Sat); 70 mg Cholesterol; 18 g Carbohydrate (3 g Fibre, 6 g Sugar); 28 g Protein; 520 mg Sodium

1 × 14 oz (398 mL) can of
diced tomatoes (with juice)

3/4 cup (175 mL) medium
pitted black olives

3 Tbsp (45 mL) half-and-half
cream

12 lemon slices

2 tsp (10 mL) chopped fresh
oregano

Stuffed Baked Salmon

Serves 8

Everyone loves a good stuffed salmon—and there's plenty of stuffing here! We've baked an extra packet of stuffing alongside the salmon to satisfy everyone's cravings.

1/3 cup (75 mL) butter

1/2 cup (125 mL) chopped celery

1/2 cup (125 mL) chopped onion

1/2 cup (125 mL) diced peeled sweet potato

9 cups (2.25 L) cubed whole-wheat bread (1 inch, 2.5 cm, pieces)

2 tsp (10 mL) dried parsley

1 tsp (5 mL) dried thyme

1 tsp (5 mL) lemon pepper

2 1/2–3 lbs (1.1–1.4 kg) whole salmon, pan ready

1/2 tsp (2 mL) lemon pepper

Melt butter in large frying pan on medium. Add celery and onion. Cook for about 5 minutes, stirring occasionally, until celery is tender-crisp.

Add sweet potato. Cook for about 3 minutes, stirring occasionally, until sweet potato starts to soften.

Add next 4 ingredients. Remove from heat. Stir until bread is coated. Arrange half of bread mixture on greased foil sheet. Wrap loosely.

Stuff remaining bread mixture into fish cavity. Tie with butcher's string or secure with metal skewers to enclose filling. Sprinkle outside of fish with second amount of lemon pepper. Place on baking sheet lined with greased foil. Place foil-wrapped stuffing on same baking sheet. Bake in 350°F (175°C) oven for about 40 minutes until fish flakes easily when tested with fork.

1 serving: 370 Calories; 18 g Total Fat (4.5 g Mono, 4 g Poly, 6 g Sat); 100 mg Cholesterol; 23 g Carbohydrate (4 g Fibre, 4 g Sugar); 33 g Protein; 380 mg Sodium

Mojo Grilled Salmon

Serves 6

This magical concoction of garlic, cumin and citrus tops grilled salmon for a truly enchanting combination! The sauce is so tasty that unused portions can be stored in the refrigerator for up to one week and used to top steamed vegetables as well.

1 tsp (5 mL) butter

2 cloves garlic, minced

Heat first amount of butter in small frying pan on medium. Add garlic. Cook for about 1 minute, stirring often, until fragrant and starting to brown.

2 Tbsp (30 mL) lime juice

2 Tbsp (30 mL) orange juice

1/4 tsp (1 mL) ground cumin

1/4 tsp (1 mL) no-salt seasoning

1/4 tsp (1 mL) pepper

1/2 cup (125 mL) butter, melted

Add next 5 ingredients. Process in blender until smooth. With motor running, add melted butter in thin stream through hole in lid until thickened.

1 tsp (5 mL) cooking oil

6 salmon steaks (5–6 oz, 140–170 g, each)

salt, sprinkle

pepper, sprinkle

Preheat gas barbecue to medium. Brush cooking oil over both sides of salmon steaks. Sprinkle with salt and pepper. Cook on greased grill for about 5 minutes per side until fish flakes easily when tested with fork.

1 1/2 tsp (7 mL) grated orange zest

2 large oranges, peeled, membrane removed and sectioned

Drizzle with butter mixture. Sprinkle with orange zest, and garnish with orange sections.

1 serving: 350 Calories; 20 g Total Fat (6 g Mono, 4.5 g Poly, 7 g Sat); 115 mg Cholesterol; 7 g Carbohydrate (1 g Fibre, 5 g Sugar); 34 g Protein; 135 mg Sodium

Citrus Soy-glazed Salmon

Serves 4

Destined to please the most refined of palates, sublime salmon is dressed to impress. A squeeze of fresh lemon further enhances the fabulous flavours. Serve with a side of grilled asparagus and cherry tomatoes.

1 cup (250 mL) grapefruit juice

1/2 cup (125 mL) sake

1/4 cup (60 mL) sugar

1/4 cup (60 mL) low-sodium soy sauce

1/4 tsp (1 mL) dried crushed chilies

2 tsp (10 mL) cornstarch

2 Tbsp (30 mL) water

2 Tbsp (30 mL) mirin

1 Tbsp (15 mL) lime juice

4 salmon fillets (4–5 oz, 113–140 g, each)

1 tsp (5 mL) grated lemon zest

Bring first 5 ingredients to a boil in a small saucepan on medium-high, stirring often. Boil, uncovered, for 8 minutes, stirring occasionally, until reduced by half.

Stir cornstarch into water until smooth and add to pan. Heat and stir for 10 minutes until thickened.

Stir in mirin and lime juice. Transfer 1/4 cup (60 mL) glaze to a small cup.

Cook fillets on a greased grill on medium-high for 2 to 3 minutes per side, brushing with glaze in pan, until fish flakes easily when tested with a fork. Transfer to a serving plate.

Drizzle with reserved glaze and sprinkle with lemon zest.

1 serving: 350 Calories; 9 g Total Fat (3 g Mono, 3.5 g Poly, 1.5 g Sat); 80 mg Cholesterol; 27 g Carbohydrate (0 g Fibre, 21 g Sugar); 30 g Protein; 680 mg Sodium

Asian dishes can often be salty. If you're watching your sodium intake, use reduced-sodium products in your cooking.

Spark Tuna

Serves 2

Beautiful red tuna with savoury relish to create a spark of enchantment in your mouth; with flavours of sun-dried tomato, scallion and balsamic. Great for blue skies and hot days.

2 tsp (10 mL) extra-virgin olive oil

1 Tbsp (15 mL) lemon juice

1 tsp (5 mL) smoked paprika

1/4 tsp (1 mL) pepper

2 × 7 oz (200 g) ahi tuna fillets (thick loin cut), patted dry

2 tsp (10 mL) extra-virgin olive oil

1 clove garlic, minced

1/2 tsp (2 mL) grated lemon zest (see Tip, page 23)

2 Tbsp (30 mL) diced celery

2 Tbsp (30 mL) thinly sliced scallion (white and green parts)

1/4 cup (60 mL) roughly chopped sun-dried tomatoes

1 tsp (5 mL) low-sodium soy sauce

1 tsp (5 mL) extra-virgin olive oil

(see next page)

On a large plate mix together first 4 ingredients to make a marinade. Add fillets to plate and rub entirely with marinade. Allow to sit at room temperature for 30 minutes.

Heat large heavy-bottomed pan over medium-high (see Tip, page 88). Add second amount of olive oil. Heat for 1 minute. Add garlic, lemon zest, celery, scallion and sun-dried tomato. Cook, stirring, for 1 to 2 minutes until vegetables to begin to soften; do not brown. Reduce heat. Stir in soy sauce and cook for 1 additional minute. Transfer relish to a small bowl.

Return pan to stove over medium-high. Add third amount of olive oil. Heat for 1 minute. Gently add fillets to pan and cook for 1 to 2 minutes. Carefully flip fillets and cook for another 1 to 2 minutes for rare or medium-rare doneness. Do not overcook. Thinner fillets will require less time to cook on each side. Transfer fish to plate. Let stand for 3 to 5 minutes.

To serve, spread a generous spoonful of relish over each
fillet. Top with fresh arugula, salt and pepper.

1 serving: 350 Calories; 14 g Total Fat (10 g Mono, 1.5 g Poly,
2 g Sat); 90 mg Cholesterol; 7 g Carbohydrate (2 g Fibre,
3 g Sugar); 48 g Protein; 720 mg Sodium

1/4 cup (60 mL) arugula

1/2 tsp (2 mL) pepper

salt, to taste

Cornmeal-crusted Halibut with Jalapeño Mayonnaise

Serves 4

Easily made in half an hour, this seafood dish partners well with potato wedges and a salad.

1 large egg

1 1/3 lbs (600 g) halibut fillets, cut into 12 equal pieces

1/4 cup (60 mL) yellow cornmeal

1/4 cup (60 mL) fine dry bread crumbs (see Tip)

1 tsp (5 mL) ground cumin

1 tsp (5 mL) ground coriander

1/2 tsp (2 mL) no-salt seasoning

1/2 tsp (2 mL) pepper

Jalapeño Mayonnaise

1/4 cup (60 mL) mayonnaise

2 Tbsp (30 mL) fat-free sour cream

2 1/2 Tbsp (37 mL) chopped pickled jalapeño peppers

2 Tbsp (30 mL) chopped fresh chives

1/2 tsp (2 mL) grated lemon zest

Lightly beat egg in medium bowl. Add fish. Gently stir to coat.

Combine next 6 ingredients in shallow dish or on waxed paper. Press fish into cornmeal mixture to coat completely. Arrange in single layer on greased baking sheet. Lightly spray fish with cooking spray. Bake in 425°F (220°C) oven for about 10 minutes, turning once, until golden and fish flakes easily when tested with fork.

Jalapeño Mayonnaise: Combine all 5 ingredients in small bowl. Makes 1/2 cup (125 mL) mayonnaise. Serve with fish.

1 serving: 360 Calories; 15 g Total Fat (8 g Mono, 4.5 g Poly, 2 g Sat); 105 mg Cholesterol; 15 g Carbohydrate (less than 1 g Fibre, less than 1 g Sugar); 35 g Protein; 350 mg Sodium

Tip

To make dry bread crumbs, remove the crusts from slices of stale or two-day-old bread. Leave the bread on the counter for a day or two until it's dry, or, if you're in a hurry, set the bread slices on a baking sheet and bake in a 200°F (95°C) oven, turning occasionally, until dry. Break the bread into pieces and process until crumbs reach the desired fineness. One slice of bread will make about 1/4 cup (60 mL) fine dry bread crumbs. Freeze extra bread crumbs in an airtight container or in a resealable plastic bag.

Blueberry Halibut

Serves 2

Thick-cut halibut splashed with flavours of sage and white balsamic, topped with a refreshing blueberry yogurt and crisp graham crackers.

1 tsp (5 mL) blueberry vinegar (or white balsamic vinegar)

1/2 tsp (2 mL) chopped fresh sage

1/4 tsp (1 mL) no-salt seasoning

1/4 tsp (1 mL) pepper

2 × 6 oz (170 g) halibut fillets (centre cut), patted dry

1/3 cup (75 mL) Greek yogurt

1/4 cup (60 mL) fresh (or frozen, thawed) blueberries, chopped

1 1/2 Tbsp (22 mL) liquid honey

1 Tbsp (15 mL) lemon juice

2 tsp (10 mL) canola oil

2 Tbsp (30 mL) graham cracker crumbs

On a large plate mix together first 4 ingredients to make a marinade. Add fillets to plate and rub entirely with marinade. Allow to sit at room temperature for 10 minutes.

Combine next 4 ingredients in small bowl. Mix loosely to create a marbled look. Set aside.

Heat large heavy-bottomed pan over high (see Tip). Add canola oil. Heat for 1 minute. Gently place each fillet in pan. Slightly reduce heat and cook for 2 to 3 minutes, until browned. Carefully flip fillets and brown other side, another 2 to 3 minutes. Then place entire pan in 400°F (200°C) oven for 8 minutes, or until fish is cooked medium-well. Remove from oven. Tent with foil. Let stand for 5 minutes.

To serve, spread a spoonful of blueberry yogurt over top of each fillet. Top with graham cracker crumbs.

1 serving: 360 Calories; 13 g Total Fat (4 g Mono, 2.5 g Poly, 3.5 g Sat); 65 mg Cholesterol; 23 g Carbohydrate (1 g Fibre, 17 g Sugar); 37 g Protein; 170 mg Sodium

Tip

Use a non-stick or well-seasoned pan to avoid the fish sticking to it. Use gentle hands when flipping fillets to avoid breaking them.

Champagne Snapper

Serves 2

A tropical sensation! Champagne-marinated snapper with a crisp coconut crust and ataulfo—also known as champagne—mango.

1/4 cup (60 mL) shredded coconut

Spread shredded coconut on large plate.

On separate large plate, mix together next 8 ingredients.

3 Tbsp (45 mL) Champagne

1 Tbsp (15 mL) lemon juice

1 Tbsp (15 mL) Dijon mustard

1 tsp (5 mL) canola oil

1 tsp (5 mL) brown sugar

1/4 tsp (1 mL) chopped fresh sage

1/4 tsp (1 mL) no-salt seasoning

1/4 tsp (1 mL) pepper

Dust cornstarch over fillets. Place fillets in Champagne mixture and turn to coat. Transfer fillets to plate with shredded coconut and turn to coat.

Heat large heavy-bottomed pan over medium-high (see Tip, page 88). Add 1 Tbsp (15 mL) butter and heat until melted. Add breaded fillets to pan and cook until they begin to brown slightly, 2 to 3 minutes. Carefully flip fillets and add 1 tsp (5 mL) butter to centre of pan. Then place entire pan in 400°F (200°C) oven for 6 to 8 minutes. Remove fillets from oven. Let stand for 3 to 5 minutes.

1 Tbsp (15 mL) cornstarch

2 × 6 oz (170 g) snapper fillets (centre cut), patted dry

1 Tbsp (15 mL) plus 1 tsp (5 mL) butter

Meanwhile, place mango in small bowl. Add second amount of lemon juice. Toss.

1 ataulfo (champagne) mango, peeled and sliced

1 Tbsp (15 mL) lemon juice

Serve fillets topped with mango and pumpkin seeds.

2 tsp (10 mL) pumpkin seeds

1 serving: 400 Calories; 14 g Total Fat (3.5 g Mono, 2 g Poly, 7 g Sat); 80 mg Cholesterol; 29 g Carbohydrate (3 g Fibre, 19 g Sugar); 36 g Protein; 250 mg Sodium

Cool Cucumber Arctic Char

Serves 2

This cold water fish is a great pair with cool cucumber. Tender baked arctic char with a mellow cream cheese spread. An excellent source of vitamins C, K and potassium.

1 English cucumber

1/8 tsp (0.5 mL) salt

2 × 5–6 oz (140–170 g) arctic char fillets, patted dry

1 Tbsp (15 mL) lemon juice

1/4 tsp (1 mL) no-salt seasoning

1/4 tsp (1 mL) pepper

1/4 cup (60 mL) light cream cheese, softened

2 Tbsp (30 mL) low-fat Greek yogurt

1 Tbsp (15 mL) lemon juice

2 black olives, minced

1 clove garlic, minced

1 Tbsp (15 mL) chopped fresh Italian parsley

1 tsp (5 mL) chopped fresh dill

1/4 tsp (1 mL) cayenne pepper

1/4 English cucumber, thinly sliced

Grate cucumber into a fine-mesh sieve. Mix salt into shredded cucumber and squeeze liquid from cucumber. Leave cucumber in sieve and return every 5 minutes to continue to squeeze liquid out.

Season char fillets with lemon juice, no-salt seasoning and pepper. Place fillets on parchment paper-lined baking sheet. Bake in 375°F (190°C) oven for 15 minutes, or until fish is cooked to medium doneness. Remove from oven. Let stand for 5 minutes.

In the meantime, whip cream cheese until fluffy. Add next 7 ingredients. Transfer grated cucumber to cutting board and roughly chop. Add to cream cheese mixture and stir until well combined.

Serve fillets with a generous spread of cream cheese mixture and a garnish of fresh cucumber slices.

1 serving: 380 Calories; 20 g Total Fat (0 g Mono, 0 g Poly, 4 g Sat); 50 mg Cholesterol; 13 g Carbohydrate (1 g Fibre, 6 g Sugar); 40 g Protein; 440 mg Sodium

Bangkok Basa

Serves 4

Eclectic and enchanting, the resplendent colours and flavours in this dish will dazzle. Serve as a main entree accompanied by rice or as one element of a multi-dish, Thai-themed dinner party.

2 tsp (10 mL) tamarind paste

1/2 cup (125 mL) water

2 Tbsp (30 mL) low-sodium soy sauce

2 Tbsp (30 mL) lime juice

2 Tbsp (30 mL) brown sugar

1 Tbsp (15 mL) cooking oil

3 cloves garlic, minced

1 1/2 tsp (7 mL) tom yum paste

1 tsp (5 mL) chili paste (sambal oelek)

1 tsp (5 mL) dried chilies

1 cup (250 mL) sliced red onion

3/4 cup (175 mL) chopped green onion (1 inch, 2.5 cm pieces)

3/4 cup (175 mL) sliced green pepper

3/4 cup (175 mL) sliced red pepper

3/4 cup (175 mL) sliced yellow pepper

(see next page)

Mix tamarind paste and water in small bowl until well combined. Let stand for 5 minutes. Stir in next 3 ingredients. Set aside.

Heat a wok or large frying pan on medium-high. Add first amount of cooking oil. Add next 4 ingredients and stir-fry for about 30 seconds until fragrant.

Add next 5 ingredients and stir-fry for about 3 minutes until vegetables start to soften. Stir in tamarind mixture and bring to a boil. Arrange on a serving plate.

Heat second amount of cooking oil in a large frying pan on medium-high. Dredge fillets in flour and cook for 2 minutes per side until golden and fish flakes easily when tested with a fork. Arrange over vegetable mixture.

1 serving: 360 Calories; 19 g Total Fat (11 g Mono, 4.5 g Poly, 2 g Sat); 10 mg Cholesterol; 30 g Carbohydrate (2 g Fibre, 12 g Sugar); 19 g Protein; 754 mg Sodium

1/4 cup (60 mL) cooking oil

1 lb (454 g) basa fillets, halved lengthwise

1/2 cup (125 mL) all-purpose flour

Temple Basa

Serves 2

An Asian-inspired dish featuring edamame beans in two different forms. Miso is a fermented soy bean paste and has been shown to have positive effects on the digestive and immune systems.

1 Tbsp (15 mL) lime juice

2 tsp (10 mL) canola oil

1/2 tsp (2 mL) chopped fresh cilantro

1/4 tsp (1 mL) pepper

2 × 8 oz (250 g) basa fillets, patted dry

2 Tbsp (30 mL) water

1 Tbsp (15 mL) lemon juice

1 Tbsp (15 mL) miso paste

2 tsp (10 mL) natural peanut butter

1 tsp (5 mL) brown sugar

1 tsp (5 mL) canola oil

3 Tbsp (45 mL) dry white wine

1/2 cup (125 mL) chopped mango

1/4 cup (60 mL) fresh edamame beans

On a large plate mix together first 4 ingredients to make a marinade. Add fillets to plate and rub entirely with marinade. Allow to sit at room temperature for 10 minutes.

Combine next 5 ingredients in small bowl. Mix to a smooth consistency. Set aside.

Preheat oven to high broil. Heat a large heavy-bottomed pan over high (see Tip, page 88). Add canola oil. Heat for 1 minute. Gently place each fillet in pan. Slightly reduce heat and cook for 2 to 3 minutes, until browned. Carefully flip fillets and brown the other side, another 2 to 3 minutes. Deglaze pan with white wine. Spoon miso glaze over fillets. Then place entire pan in oven on bottom rack for 5 minutes. The miso glaze should begin to darken and caramelize. Remove from oven.

Add mango and edamame to pan. Cover. Let stand for 5 minutes. Serve fillets with warmed edamame beans and mango.

1 serving: 370 Calories; 13 g Total Fat (4 g Mono, 2 g Poly, 2 g Sat); 20 mg Cholesterol; 22 g Carbohydrate (3 g Fibre, 11 g Sugar); 38 g Protein; 1250 mg Sodium

Scallop and Artichoke Risotto

Serves 6

Rich and creamy risotto is always an elegant main course—perfect for serving company. Tender shrimp, tangy artichoke, and a lovely herb flavour make this recipe unforgettable.

6 cups (1.5 L) prepared low-sodium vegetable broth

Bring broth to a boil in medium saucepan. Reduce heat to low. Cover to keep hot.

1 Tbsp (15 mL) cooking oil

1 cup (250 mL) chopped onion

Heat cooking oil in large saucepan on medium. Add onion. Cook for about 5 minutes, stirring often, until onion is softened.

1 1/2 cups (375 mL) arborio rice

1 cup (250 mL) grated zucchini (with peel)

1 clove garlic, minced

1/4 tsp (1 mL) coarsely ground pepper

Add next 4 ingredients. Heat and stir for about 1 minute until rice is coated and garlic is fragrant. Add 1 cup (250 mL) of hot broth, stirring constantly until broth is absorbed. Repeat with remaining broth, 1 cup (250 mL) at a time, until broth is absorbed and rice is tender and creamy.

2 tsp (10 mL) olive oil

1 lb (454 g) small bay scallops

Heat olive oil in medium frying pan on medium. Add scallops. Cook for about 2 minutes. Add scallops to rice mixture.

1 × 14 oz (398 mL) can of artichoke hearts, drained and quartered

Add artichoke hearts. Stir. Cook for about 3 minutes, stirring constantly, until heated through.

2 cups (500 mL) halved grape tomatoes

3 oz (85 g) goat (chèvre) cheese, cut up

3 Tbsp (45 mL) chopped fresh parsley

1 Tbsp (15 mL) white wine vinegar

Add remaining 4 ingredients. Stir gently. Serve.

1 serving: 370 Calories; 8 g Total Fat (3 g Mono, 1.5 g Poly, 2.5 g Sat); 45 mg Cholesterol; 48 g Carbohydrate (3 g Fibre, 5 g Sugar); 25 g Protein; 750 mg Sodium

Crab and Cauli on Rye

Serves 2

Creamy crab and cauliflower with tender cooked leek over rye toast. A great source of calcium and B12.

1 lb (454 g) Alaskan crab legs

Crack apart crab legs and remove meat; roughly chop meat. Inspect meat to ensure there is no shell or tendons. Set aside.

1 Tbsp (15 mL) butter

3/4 cup (175 mL) cauliflower florets

1/2 cup (125 mL) sliced leek (bulb and lower leaf portion)

1/4 cup (60 mL) dry white wine

Heat large heavy-bottomed pan over medium-high. Add butter and heat until melted. Add cauliflower, leek and crab. Cook, stirring, until vegetables begin to soften, 2 to 3 minutes. Stir in wine. Reduce heat to low. Partially cover and cook for 8 to 10 minutes, until liquid has evaporated.

1/3 cup (75 mL) table cream (18%)

1 Tbsp (15 mL) lemon juice

2 tsp (10 mL) grainy mustard

1/4 tsp (1 mL) pepper

1/8 tsp (0.5 mL) ground cloves

Stir in cream, lemon juice, mustard, pepper and cloves. Simmer for 1 to 2 minutes to infuse flavours.

While sauce is simmering, toast rye bread.

2 slices of rye bread

Spoon crab mixture generously over toasted rye. Garnish with arugula. Sprinkle with paprika, salt and pepper.

1 serving: 350 Calories; 15 g Total Fat (4 g Mono, 1 g Poly, 8 g Sat); 80 mg Cholesterol; 26 g Carbohydrate (4 g Fibre, 2 g Sugar); 22 g Protein; 1150 mg Sodium

1/4 cup (60 mL) arugula

1 tsp (5 mL) paprika

salt, to taste

pepper, to taste

Ruby Red Lobster Tail

Serves 2

Here lies a simple yet delicious recipe for lobster tail. Impress your guests at your next dinner party with this low-calorie delight.

2 × 8–9 oz (225–250 g) lobster tails

1 tsp (5 mL) paprika

1/4 tsp (1 mL) chopped fresh tarragon

1/4 tsp (1 mL) pepper

2 Tbsp (30 mL) unsalted butter, melted

1 Tbsp (15 mL) lemon juice

2 cups (500 mL) water

3 Tbsp (45 mL) lemon juice

Using your kitchen shears, make a single cut down the back of 1 lobster shell. Gently peel shell away from lobster meat. Pull meat through the cut, leaving it attached only at the very tip of the tail. Allow lobster meat to rest on top of shell. Repeat with other lobster tail (see Tip).

Place lobster tails in medium oven-safe pot. Dust meat of each tail with paprika, tarragon and pepper, then drizzle butter and lemon juice over top.

Combine water and second amount of lemon juice. Carefully pour lemon water into pot; do not pour directly over top of lobster tails. Cover with a tight-fitting lid (or foil). Place entire pot in 425°F (220°C) oven and cook for 7 to 8 minutes, depending on size of lobster tails. At 2 minute intervals, remove pot from oven and spoon lemon water over top of tails to keep them moist. When cooked, remove pot from oven. Let stand, covered, for 3 to 5 minutes. Just before serving, generously spoon cooking liquid over top of lobster meat.

1 serving: 360 Calories; 14 g Total Fat (3 g Mono, 0.5 g Poly, 8 g Sat); 290 mg Cholesterol; 4 g Carbohydrate (less than 1 g Fibre, 0 g Sugar); 51 g Protein; 940 mg Sodium

Tip

Don't rush yourself when cutting the shell and removing the lobster meat. Gently pull the meat from the shell to avoid tearing the meat and pricking your fingers.

Having the shell present in the pot acts as both a steamer and flavour enhancer. It keeps the lobster above the water level and adds flavour to the cooking liquid used to keep the meat moist.

Savoury Pork Roast

Serves 12

This dressy dish is easy to serve and a perfect accompaniment or alternative to roast turkey.

1/4 cup (60 mL) olive oil

1/4 cup (60 mL) chopped fresh parsley

1/4 cup (60 mL) diced onion

3 cloves garlic, minced

2 Tbsp (30 mL) honey Dijon mustard

2 tsp (10 mL) lemon pepper

1 tsp (5 mL) dried sage

1/2 tsp (2 mL) ground coriander

3–4 lbs (1.4–1.8 kg) boneless pork loin roast

Mushroom Sauce

3 Tbsp (45 mL) butter

3 Tbsp (45 mL) olive oil

6 cups (1.5 L) sliced brown mushrooms

1/4 cup (60 mL) all-purpose flour

1/2 tsp (2 mL) dried sage

1/2 tsp (2 mL) salt

1/4 tsp (1 mL) pepper

(see next page)

Combine first 8 ingredients in small bowl.

Score 1/4 inch (6 mm) deep diamond pattern in fat on top of roast. Rub parsley mixture evenly over entire surface of roast. Wrap with plastic wrap. Chill for at least 6 hours or overnight. Place roast on greased wire rack set in 9 × 13 inch (23 × 33 cm) pan. Cook, uncovered, in 400°F (200°C) oven for 30 minutes. Reduce heat to 325°F (160°C). Cover roast loosely with foil if browning too quickly. Cook for another 1 to 1 1/4 hours until meat thermometer inserted into thickest part of roast reads 160°F (70°C). Transfer roast to cutting board. Tent with foil. Let stand for at least 10 minutes. Pour juices from pan through sieve into small bowl. Set aside.

Mushroom Sauce: Heat butter and olive oil in large frying pan on medium-high until butter is melted. Add mushrooms. Cook for about 10 minutes, stirring occasionally, until mushrooms are browned and liquid is evaporated. Reduce heat to medium.

Add next 4 ingredients. Stir well.

Gradually add sherry, broth and pan juices, stirring constantly until smooth. Increase heat to medium-high. Heat and stir for about 5 minutes until boiling and thickened. Makes about 3 1/4 cups (800 mL) sauce.

Slice roast and arrange on large serving platter. Drizzle 1 cup (250 mL) sauce over roast slices. Garnish with parsley and lemon. Serve with remaining sauce.

1 serving: 350 Calories; 19 g Total Fat (10 g Mono, 2 g Poly, 6 g Sat); 90 mg Cholesterol; 5 g Carbohydrate (less than 1 g Fibre, 1 g Sugar); 34 g Protein; 320 mg Sodium

3/4 cup (175 mL) dry sherry

2 cups (500 mL) prepared chicken broth

sprigs of fresh parsley, for garnish

lemon slices, for garnish

Braised Pork Loin with Cream Gravy

Serves 8

In cooking, just as in fashion, what's old is new again. Get out your grandmother's pressure cooker, and make something delicious.

1/4 cup (60 mL) all-purpose flour

1 tsp (5 mL) paprika

1/2 tsp (2 mL) salt

1/2 tsp (2 mL) pepper

2 1/4 lbs (1 kg) boneless pork loin (or butt) roast, trimmed of fat, rolled and tied

2 Tbsp (30 mL) olive oil

2 thick slices of double-smoked (or European) bacon (about 2 oz, 57 g), chopped

2 celery ribs, diced

1 medium carrot, diced

1 small onion, diced

2 cloves garlic, minced

(see next page)

Combine first 4 ingredients in shallow bowl. Roll roast in flour mixture to coat completely. If desired, reserve any remaining flour mixture to thicken gravy later.

Heat olive oil in pressure cooker on medium-high. Brown roast well all over. Remove roast to large plate. Set aside.

Add bacon to pressure cooker. Cook for 5 minutes until just cooked.

Add next 4 ingredients. Cook for 5 minutes until vegetables are tender.

Add next 5 ingredients. Stir. Return roast to cooker. Lock lid in place. Bring up to pressure on high heat. Reduce heat to medium-low just to maintain pressure. Cook for 40 minutes. Release pressure. Remove lid. Transfer roast to cutting board and tent with foil to keep warm. Put vegetables and bacon mixture with juices in blender or food processor. Process until smooth. Return to pressure cooker. Heat and stir on medium until hot.

For a richer gravy, combine sour cream and reserved flour mixture in small bowl. Whisk into vegetable mixture. Simmer, uncovered, until thickened. Season with salt and pepper. Stir. Makes about 1 1/2 cups (375 mL) gravy. Slice roast. Serve with gravy.

1 serving: 350 Calories; 20 g Total Fat (9 g Mono, 2 g Poly, 6 g Sat); 95 mg Cholesterol; 8 g Carbohydrate (1 g Fibre, 2 g Sugar); 30 g Protein; 480 mg Sodium

1 cup (250 mL) prepared low-sodium chicken broth

3/4 cup (175 mL) dry white wine

2 Tbsp (30 mL) tomato paste (see Tip, page 38)

1 tsp (5 mL) paprika

1 tsp (5 mL) dried thyme

1/4 cup (60 mL) sour cream (optional)

salt, to taste

pepper, to taste

Cranberry Apple Pork Roast

Serves 12

If you think cranberries are just for Thanksgiving turkey, then you must try this tender pork roast dressed up with a bright cranberry sauce spiced with ginger, jalapeño pepper and lime.

4–4 1/2 lbs (1.8–2 kg) boneless pork loin roast

1/4 tsp (1 mL) salt

1/4 tsp (1 mL) pepper

Cranberry Apple Sauce

3 cups (750 mL) frozen (or fresh) cranberries

2 cups (500 mL) chopped peeled cooking apple (such as McIntosh)

1/2 cup (125 mL) liquid honey

3 Tbsp (45 mL) frozen concentrated apple juice

2 Tbsp (30 mL) chopped jalapeño pepper (see Tip)

1 Tbsp (15 mL) grated ginger root

1 tsp (5 mL) grated lime zest

Place roast in large roasting pan. Sprinkle with salt and pepper. Cook, uncovered, in 400°F (200°C) oven for 30 minutes. Reduce heat to 325°F (160°C). Cook, uncovered, for about 45 minutes until meat thermometer inserted into thickest part of roast reads at least 155°F (68°C) or more depending on desired doneness. Transfer to cutting board. Tent with foil. Let stand for 10 minutes. Cut roast into thin slices. Arrange on serving platter.

Cranberry Apple Sauce: Combine all 7 ingredients in medium saucepan. Bring to a boil. Reduce heat to medium. Simmer, uncovered, for about 10 minutes, stirring occasionally, until cranberries are soft. Makes about 3 cups (750 mL) sauce. Spoon over pork and serve.

1 serving: 350 Calories; 9 g Total Fat (4 g Mono, 1 g Poly, 3 g Sat); 95 mg Cholesterol; 27 g Carbohydrate (2 g Fibre, 22 g Sugar); 37 g Protein; 130 mg Sodium

Tip

Wear gloves when chopping chili peppers, and avoid touching your eyes.

Whisky Molasses-glazed Ham

Serves 12

For impressive entrees, you can't beat a whole roasted ham, especially with a sweet, smoky and peppery glaze. Save the bone to make flavourful soup stock.

Whisky Molasses Glaze

1/2 cup (125 mL) frozen concentrated orange juice, thawed

1/3 cup (75 mL) peach jam

1/4 cup (60 mL) molasses

3 Tbsp (45 mL) whisky

2 Tbsp (30 mL) Dijon mustard

1 1/2 tsp (7 mL) coarsely ground pepper

8–10 lbs (3.6–4.5 kg) partially cooked skinless ham (bone-in), fat trimmed to 1/4 inch (6 mm) thick

Whisky Molasses Glaze: Combine all 6 ingredients in small saucepan. Bring to a boil on medium. Reduce heat to medium-low. Simmer, uncovered, for about 15 minutes until thickened. Makes about 1 cup (250 mL) glaze.

Place ham in large roasting pan. Cook, covered, in 325°F (160°C) oven for about 2 hours until meat thermometer inserted in thickest part of ham reads 130°F (55°C). Brush with Whisky Molasses Glaze. Cook, uncovered, for about 1 hour, brushing with glaze every 15 minutes, until meat thermometer inserted into thickest part of ham reads 160°F (70°C). Transfer to cutting board. Tent with foil. Let stand for 10 minutes. Brush with pan juices. Slice ham and serve.

1 serving: 390 Calories; 14 g Total Fat (7 g Mono, 1.5 g Poly, 4.5 g Sat); 140 mg Cholesterol; 16 g Carbohydrate (0 g Fibre, 14 g Sugar); 45 g Protein; 140 mg Sodium

Grilled Butterflied Lamb with Pomegranate Reduction

Serves 8

The reduction of pomegranate not only intensifies the flavour of the fruit, originally from the Middle East, but also balances the rich earthiness of the lamb, creating a feast of pleasing contrasts for your guests.

3 cups (750 mL) pomegranate juice

Gently boil pomegranate juice in a saucepan on medium until reduced to about 1/2 cup (125 mL).

3 lbs (1.4 kg) boneless leg of lamb roast, butterflied, fat and sinews trimmed (see Tip)

2 Tbsp (30 mL) olive oil

Pound butterflied lamb between 2 sheets of plastic wrap to an even thickness. Score lightly on both sides and brush with olive oil.

1/4 cup (60 mL) chopped fresh oregano

5 cloves garlic, minced

2 tsp (10 mL) seasoned salt

2 tsp (10 mL) coarsely ground pepper

Combine next 4 ingredients and rub over lamb. Chill, covered, for 2 hours. Grill on direct medium heat for about 12 minutes per side until internal temperature reaches 145°F (63°C) for medium-rare or until lamb reaches desired doneness. Transfer to cutting board. Tent with foil. Let stand for 10 minutes. Cut lamb diagonally, across the grain, into thin slices.

sprigs of fresh oregano, for garnish

Serve with pomegranate reduction. Garnish with oregano.

1 serving: 400 Calories; 22 g Total Fat (9 g Mono, 2 g Poly, 9 g Sat); 110 mg Cholesterol; 17 g Carbohydrate (1 g Fibre, 14 g Sugar); 33 g Protein; 520 mg Sodium

Tip

To butterfly lamb, cut horizontally along roast, almost but not quite through to other side. Open flat.

Pineapple Lamb Kabobs with Spiced Yogurt

Serves 4

Lamb is a great choice for indoor or outdoor grilling. Serve these colourful Mediterranean-style kabobs with extra flavourful spiced yogurt.

1 1/2 lbs (680 g) lamb tenderloin (or medallions), cut into 1 inch (2.5 cm) cubes

1/4 cup (60 mL) balsamic vinegar

2 cloves garlic, crushed

1 1/2 Tbsp (22 mL) olive oil

2 tsp (10 mL) whole black peppercorns, cracked

2 cups (500 mL) cubed fresh pineapple

2 cups (500 mL) cubed red pepper

(see next page)

Toss first 5 ingredients together in medium bowl to coat.

Alternate lamb, pineapple and red pepper on skewers. Grill or broil for about 10 minutes, turning occasionally, until lamb reaches desired doneness.

Spiced Yogurt: Combine all 5 ingredients in small bowl. Mix well. Makes 2 cups (500 mL) spiced yogurt. Serve with kabobs.

1 serving: 380 Calories; 14 g Total Fat (7 g Mono, 1 g Poly, 4 g Sat); 110 mg Cholesterol; 24 g Carbohydrate (3 g Fibre, 17 g Sugar); 39 g Protein; 150 mg Sodium

If using wooden skewers, remember to soak them in water before using them.

Spiced Yogurt

1 cup (250 mL) low-fat plain
yogurt

1/2 cup (125 mL) diced red
onion

1/4 cup (60 mL) diced
English cucumber

1/4 cup (60 mL) chopped
fresh cilantro

1 tsp (5 mL) ground cumin

Pork Noisette

Serves 4

The French give diminutives to their favourite things: both hazelnuts and small, round, tender slices of meat are termed noisette, from noix, or nuts. The food may be petite, but the taste is tremendous!

2 Tbsp (30 mL) butter

1 Tbsp (15 mL) extra-virgin olive oil

1 Tbsp (15 mL) honey

1/2 cup (125 mL) sliced hazelnuts

2 Tbsp (30 mL) dry white wine

1 lb (454 g) pork tenderloin, trimmed of fat and cut into 8 slices

1 Tbsp (15 mL) extra-virgin olive oil

salt, sprinkle

1 tsp (5 mL) chopped fresh thyme

1 tsp (5 mL) grated orange zest

pepper, sprinkle

Melt butter in a frying pan on medium. Add first amount of olive oil, honey and hazelnuts and cook for 3 to 4 minutes, stirring often, until golden.

Add wine. Heat, stirring, until evaporated. Remove from heat, leaving hazelnut mixture in pan.

Brush pork slices with second amount of olive oil. Sprinkle with salt. Grill on direct medium-high heat for about 3 minutes per side until internal temperature reaches 160°F (70°C). Transfer to plate. Tent with foil. Let stand for 5 minutes.

Return hazelnut mixture to medium heat. Add remaining 3 ingredients. Heat and stir for 1 minute. Serve with pork.

1 serving: 350 Calories; 25 g Total Fat (16 g Mono, 2.5 g Poly, 6 g Sat); 80 mg Cholesterol; 7 g Carbohydrate (1 g Fibre, 5 g Sugar); 25 g Protein; 75 mg Sodium

Prosciutto Pork Mignon with Parsley Cilantro Crema

Serves 6

Ribbons of prosciutto wrap superbly seasoned slices of tenderloin for a magnificent meal. The tangy sauce adds vibrancy to both the plate and the palate.

1 cup (250 mL) fresh flat-leaf parsley

1/2 cup (125 mL) fresh cilantro

1/4 cup (60 mL) olive oil

3 Tbsp (45 mL) lime juice

2 cloves garlic, minced

1 tsp (5 mL) ground cumin

1 tsp (5 mL) sugar

1/2 tsp (2 mL) no-salt seasoning

1/2 tsp (2 mL) pepper

1/2 cup (125 mL) light sour cream

2 pork tenderloins (about 1 lb, 454 g, each), ends trimmed

1 1/2 tsp (7 mL) ground cumin

1 1/2 tsp (7 mL) ground coriander

1 1/2 tsp (7 mL) chili powder

1/2 tsp (2 mL) sugar

1/4 tsp (1 mL) pepper

1/8 tsp (0.5 mL) no-salt seasoning

12 prosciutto slices

In a blender or food processor, process first 9 ingredients until smooth. Add sour cream and process until just combined. Serve at room temperature.

Cut tenderloins crosswise into 6 slices each, about 1 1/2 inches (3.8 cm) thick. Combine next 6 ingredients and rub on pork slices.

Fold prosciutto slices in half lengthwise and wrap 1 slice around each pork slice, overlapping if necessary. Thread pork onto skewers, leaving a 1 inch (2.5 cm) space between portions. Grill on direct medium-high heat for 5 to 6 minutes per side until internal temperature reaches 160°F (70°C). Serve with parsley mixture.

1 serving: 400 Calories; 24 g Total Fat (11 g Mono, 2 g Poly, 7 g Sat); 130 mg Cholesterol; 5 g Carbohydrate (1 g Fibre, 1 g Sugar); 42 g Protein; 660 mg Sodium

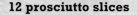

Lime Pork Chops with Chili Cilantro Butter

Serves 6

Mild-tasting pork is perfect with the jazzy taste of the accompanying chili and herb butter. When grilling the red pepper for the Chili Cilantro Butter, grill extra red peppers, red onion wedges and some zucchini slices to serve with the pork chops. Add quick-to-make buttered couscous and your guests won't know how easy it was to plan this meal.

Chili Cilantro Butter

1 medium red pepper, quartered and seeded

1/2 cup (125 mL) butter, softened

2 small red chili peppers, diced (see Tip, page 108)

1/2 cup (125 mL) chopped fresh cilantro

1/4 tsp (1 mL) salt

3 cloves garlic, crushed

1/4 cup diced onion

1 Tbsp (15 mL) grated lime zest

3 Tbsp (45 mL) lime juice

3 Tbsp (45 mL) tequila

1 Tbsp (15 mL) cooking oil

3 Tbsp (45 mL) brown sugar

1 1/2 tsp (7 mL) pepper

6 boneless pork loin chops (1 inch, 2.5 cm, thick)

Chili Cilantro Butter: Preheat grill to medium-high. Grill red pepper, skin side down, for 8 to 10 minutes until skin is blistered and blackened. Place in bowl. Cover with plastic wrap. Let stand for 10 minutes until cool enough to handle. Remove and discard skin. Dice pepper.

Combine next 4 ingredients in small bowl. Add red pepper. Mix well. Makes 3/4 cup (175 mL) butter. Spread butter mixture into 6 inch (15 cm) circle on waxed paper. Chill for 30 minutes until hard. Cut into 6 wedges.

Combine next 8 ingredients in large bowl or resealable plastic bag. Add pork. Turn to coat. Cover or seal. Marinate in refrigerator for 30 minutes. Preheat grill to medium-high. Cook chops on lightly greased grill for 6 to 8 minutes per side until chops are just tender. Do not overcook. To serve, place chops on individual serving plates. Top with wedge of Chili Cilantro Butter.

1 serving: 350 Calories; 23 g Total Fat (8 g Mono, 2 g Poly, 12 g Sat); 90 mg Cholesterol; 10 g Carbohydrate (less than 1 g Fibre, 8 g Sugar); 20 g Protein; 250 mg Sodium

Port Wine Chops with Figs

Serves 6

Gather around the table for sophisticated yet family-friendly flavours—pepper-speckled pork chops with a sweet port and fig glaze. Serve these richly flavoured chops with rice pilaf and a salad.

6 bone-in pork chops, trimmed of fat

1/2 tsp (2 mL) salt

1 tsp (5 mL) coarsely ground pepper

1 Tbsp (15 mL) cooking oil

1 tsp (5 mL) cooking oil

2 Tbsp (30 mL) diced red onion

1 cup (250 mL) port wine

1/4 cup (60 mL) red wine vinegar

12 dried figs, quartered

3/4 tsp (4 mL) chopped fresh rosemary

3 Tbsp (45 mL) half-and-half cream

1/2 tsp (2 mL) cornstarch

Sprinkle both sides of pork chops with salt and pepper. Heat first amount of cooking oil in large frying pan on medium. Cook chops, in 2 batches, for 4 to 5 minutes per side until no longer pink inside. Transfer to serving platter. Tent with foil to keep warm.

Add second amount of cooking oil to same frying pan. Add onion. Cook for about 2 minutes, stirring often, until softened.

Add next 4 ingredients. Heat and stir until boiling. Boil gently, uncovered, for about 5 minutes until liquid is reduced by half.

Stir cream into cornstarch in small cup until smooth. Add to fig mixture. Heat and stir for about 1 minute until boiling and thickened. Serve with pork chops.

1 serving: 350 Calories; 17 g Total Fat (8 g Mono, 2.5 g Poly, 5 g Sat); 65 mg Cholesterol; 18 g Carbohydrate (2 g Fibre, 12 g Sugar); 21 g Protein; 250 mg Sodium

Pork Chops with Creamed Balsamic Leeks

Serves 4

Among the most beautiful of all the onions, leeks are also the most versatile. Their flavour is mild, and their green colour brings extra nutrients to the table. Creamed leeks are a classic with pork chops, but a little white balsamic vinegar adds a whole new layer of flavour.

1 Tbsp (15 mL) grape seed oil

4 boneless pork loin chops

1/2 tsp (2 mL) salt

1/2 tsp (2 mL) pepper

2 Tbsp (30 mL) butter

6 leeks, cut lengthwise into 1/2 inch (12 mm) wide strips

3 Tbsp (45 mL) dry white wine

1/4 cup (60 mL) white balsamic vinegar

2 Tbsp (30 mL) whipping cream

Heat grape seed oil in large frying pan on medium-high. Lightly sprinkle pork chops on both sides with salt and pepper. Add chops to pan and cook until golden brown and just barely pink inside, 3 to 4 minutes on each side. Transfer to cutting board. Tent with foil. Let stand for 10 minutes.

Meanwhile, melt butter in same pan over medium-low. Add leeks and cook, stirring occasionally, until they begin to soften, about 5 minutes. Add white wine and cook until almost evaporated, scraping brown bits from sides of pan. Add balsamic vinegar and remaining salt and pepper; cook until reduced by half, about 5 minutes more. Stir in cream and cook just to heat through. Divide into 4 equal portions. Pile most of each portion of leeks on a serving plate, lean a pork chop on top and pile remaining leeks on top of that.

1 serving: 350 Calories; 18 g Total Fat (6 g Mono, 3.5 g Poly, 8 g Sat); 70 mg Cholesterol; 21 g Carbohydrate (4 g Fibre, 7 g Sugar); 22 g Protein; 390 mg Sodium

Leeks need to be washed well—slice them lengthwise and run them under the tap so the water washes away the gritty dirt that might have accumulated in the layers.

Ginger Pork

Serves 4

If you love the taste of ginger, this dish is for you. The slight heat from the cayenne pepper will linger in your mouth. Serve with rice noodles.

2 Tbsp (30 mL) sesame oil

1/4 cup (60 mL) cornstarch

1 lb (454 g) boneless pork loin, cut julienne

1/4 tsp (1 mL) cayenne pepper

1 Tbsp (15 mL) cooking oil

2 medium carrots, cut julienne

2 Tbsp (30 mL) grated ginger root

1 medium onion, cut lengthwise into slivers

2 Tbsp (30 mL) honey

1 Tbsp (15 mL) cooking oil

2 Tbsp (30 mL) lime juice

3 Tbsp (45 mL) Indonesian sweet (or thick) soy sauce

chopped fresh cilantro, for garnish

sliced green onion, for garnish

Stir sesame oil into cornstarch in medium bowl. Add pork and cayenne pepper. Stir until pork is coated. Let stand for 15 minutes.

Heat wok or large frying pan on medium-high. Add first amount of cooking oil. Add carrot, ginger and onion. Stir-fry for about 5 minutes until golden. Add honey. Stir-fry for about 1 minute. Transfer to bowl.

Add second amount of cooking oil to hot wok. Add pork mixture. Stir-fry for about 3 minutes, keeping pork pieces separate, until browned and no longer pink inside. Add carrot mixture. Stir. Add lime juice and soy sauce. Stir-fry for about 1 minute until pork is coated.

Sprinkle with cilantro and green onion. Serve.

1 serving: 360 Calories; 17 g Total Fat (8 g Mono, 4.5 g Poly, 2.5 g Sat); 65 mg Cholesterol; 23 g Carbohydrate (1 g Fibre, 11 g Sugar); 28 g Protein; 530 mg Sodium

Rack of Lamb with Kiwi Relish

Serves 2

This marinated rack of lamb with tangy kiwi and mint relish is simple to prepare and elegant to serve. A lovely combination of classic flavours with a modern twist.

1 clove garlic, minced

1/2 tsp (2 mL) grated lemon zest

1/4 tsp (1 mL) crushed dried rosemary

pepper, sprinkle

1 tsp (5 mL) lemon juice

1 Tbsp (15 mL) olive oil

1 1/4 lbs (560 g) rack of lamb, trimmed of fat

(see next page)

Combine first 4 ingredients in small dish until paste-like consistency. Stir in lemon juice and olive oil.

Rub garlic mixture on all sides of lamb. Place lamb in resealable plastic bag. Chill for several hours or overnight. Place lamb, meaty side down, on wire rack in shallow baking dish. Bake in 475°F (240°C) oven for 12 to 15 minutes. Reduce heat to 400°F (200°C). Turn lamb over. Bake for 20 to 30 minutes until desired doneness.

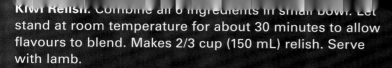

Kiwi Relish. Combine all 6 ingredients in small bowl. Let stand at room temperature for about 30 minutes to allow flavours to blend. Makes 2/3 cup (150 mL) relish. Serve with lamb.

1 serving: *390 Calories; 21 g Total Fat (9 g Mono, 1.5 g Poly, 8 g Sat); 105 mg Cholesterol; 26 g Carbohydrate (5 g Fibre, 15 g Sugar); 29 g Protein; 95 mg Sodium*

Kiwi Relish

3 medium kiwi fruit, peeled and coarsely chopped

2 Tbsp (30 mL) lime juice

1 Tbsp (15 mL) chopped fresh mint leaves

1 Tbsp (15 mL) sliced green onion

1 tsp (5 mL) sugar

salt, sprinkle

Greek Peasant Parcels

Serves 6

Harvest ingredients are put to good use in this rustic take on a popular Greek dish called Bandit's Lamb. Serve with plenty of crusty white bread or fresh pita for dipping.

1 1/2 lbs (680 g) boneless leg of lamb, trimmed of fat, cut into 1 1/2 inch (3.8 cm) pieces

2 cups (500 mL) chopped onion

2 cups (500 mL) chopped tomato

1 1/2 cups (375 mL) chopped celery root

1 1/2 cups (375 mL) chopped parsnip

1 1/2 cups (375 mL) chopped peeled potato

1 cup (250 mL) crumbled feta cheese

1/4 cup (60 mL) lemon juice

3 Tbsp (45 mL) butter, melted

2 Tbsp (30 mL) chopped fresh oregano

1 Tbsp (15 mL) chopped fresh rosemary

3 cloves garlic, thinly sliced

1/4 tsp (1 mL) no-salt seasoning

1 tsp (5 mL) coarsely ground pepper

Combine all 14 ingredients in extra-large bowl. Cut 6 sheets of heavy-duty (or double layer of regular) foil about 14 inches (35 cm) long. Spoon lamb mixture in centre of each sheet. Fold edges of foil together over mixture to enclose. Fold ends to seal completely. Arrange packets, seam-side up, on ungreased baking sheet. Bake in 325°F (160°C) oven for about 2 hours until lamb and vegetables are tender. Makes 6 parcels.

1 serving: 360 Calories; 17 g Total Fat (5 g Mono, 1 g Poly, 10 g Sat); 110 mg Cholesterol; 22 g Carbohydrate (5 g Fibre, 6 g Sugar); 29 g Protein; 430 mg Sodium

Lamb and White Bean Stew

Serves 6

Mint is the secret ingredient that pulls together all the complex, hearty spices in this delicious lamb stew.

3 cups (750 mL) sliced carrot, 1/2 inch (12 mm) thick

2 large fennel bulbs (white part only), thinly sliced

1 Tbsp (15 mL) cooking oil

1 1/2 lbs (680 g) stewing lamb

1/4 cup (60 mL) dry red wine

1 tsp (5 mL) cooking oil

2 cups (500 mL) thinly sliced onion

2 cloves garlic, minced

4 whole green cardamom, bruised (see Tip)

1 cinnamon stick (4 inches, 10 cm)

2 tsp (10 mL) grated ginger root

3/4 tsp (4 mL) no-salt seasoning

1/2 tsp (2 mL) dried crushed chilies

1/2 tsp (2 mL) ground cumin

(see next page)

Layer carrot and fennel, in order given, in 4 to 5 quart (4 to 5 L) slow cooker.

Heat first amount of cooking oil in large frying pan on medium-high. Add lamb. Cook for about 5 minutes, stirring occasionally, until browned. Deglaze pan with red wine and cook, stirring, until almost evaporated. Transfer lamb to slow cooker. Reduce heat to medium.

Add second amount of cooking oil to same frying pan. Add onion and garlic. Cook for 5 to 10 minutes, stirring often, until onion is softened.

Add next 6 ingredients. Heat and stir for 1 to 2 minutes until fragrant.

Slowly add broth and apple juice, stirring constantly and scraping any brown bits from bottom of pan. Add beans. Stir. Pour over lamb. Cook, covered, on Low for 8 to 9 hours or on High for 4 to 4 1/2 hours. Remove and discard cinnamon stick and cardamom. Transfer to serving bowl.

Sprinkle with mint. Makes about 8 cups (2 L).

1 serving: 350 Calories; 10 g Total Fat (4.5 g Mono, 1.5 g Poly, 2.5 g Sat); 75 mg Cholesterol; 34 g Carbohydrate (11 g Fibre, 8 g Sugar); 30 g Protein; 420 mg Sodium

Tip

To bruise cardamom, pound pods with a mallet or press with the flat side of a wide knife to "bruise," or crack them open slightly.

1 cup (250 mL) prepared
low-sodium beef broth

1/2 cup (125 mL) apple
juice

2 × 14 oz (398 mL) cans of
navy beans, rinsed and
drained

1/4 cup (60 mL) chopped
fresh mint

Spinach Pesto Primavera

Serves 4

You'll want to use the freshest seasonal vegetables for this dish. The leftover pesto can be stored in the refrigerator for up to three days.

Spinach Pesto

1 cup (250 mL) fresh basil leaves, lightly packed

1 cup (250 mL) fresh spinach leaves, lightly packed

3 Tbsp (45 mL) olive oil

3 Tbsp (45 mL) pine nuts, toasted (see Tip, page 64)

3 cloves garlic

1/4 tsp (1 mL) no-salt seasoning

1/2 cup (125 mL) grated light Parmesan cheese

Pasta Primavera

12 oz (340 g) linguine

1/4 cup (60 mL) butter

3/4 cup (175 mL) chopped green pepper

3/4 cup (175 mL) chopped red pepper

3/4 cup (175 mL) chopped orange pepper

3/4 cup (175 mL) chopped yellow pepper

(see next page)

Spinach Pesto: Process first 6 ingredients in blender until smooth. Transfer to small bowl. Add Parmesan cheese. Mix well. Makes about 1 cup (250 mL) pesto.

Pasta Primavera: Cook pasta according to package directions. Drain.

Melt butter in large saucepan on medium. Add next 5 ingredients. Cook for 3 to 4 minutes until tender. Deglaze pan with white wine. Cook, stirring, until almost evaporated.

Add 1/2 cup (125 mL) Spinach Pesto. Cook for 3 minutes. Add next 3 ingredients. Cook for 5 minutes. Add linguine and toss until coated. Remove from heat.

Sprinkle with pine nuts and basil. Serve.

1 serving: 350 Calories; 27 g Total Fat (11 g Mono, 4 g Poly, 4.5 g Sat); 30 mg Cholesterol; 49 g Carbohydrate (5 g Fibre, 6 g Sugar); 17 g Protein; 730 mg Sodium

1/2 cup (125 mL) sliced
fresh white mushrooms

1/4 cup (60 mL) dry white
wine

1 cup (250 mL) grape
tomatoes

1/2 cup (125 mL) pitted
kalamata olives

3 Tbsp (45 mL) grated light
Parmesan cheese

3 Tbsp (45 mL) pine nuts

chopped fresh basil, for
garnish (optional)

Cheesy Garden Macaroni

Serves 8

This fusion of two classic dishes—macaroni and cheese and vegetables au gratin—creates an attractive, crumb-topped casserole full of vegetables harvested from the garden.

10 cups (2.5 L) water

1 tsp (5 mL) salt

2 cups (500 mL) elbow macaroni

1 cup (250 mL) sliced carrot

Combine water and salt in Dutch oven. Bring to a boil. Add pasta and carrot. Cook, uncovered, for 6 minutes until carrot is tender-crisp.

1 cup (250 mL) chopped broccoli

1 cup (250 mL) chopped cauliflower

1 cup (250 mL) frozen corn

Add next 3 ingredients. Bring to a boil. Cook, uncovered, for about 3 minutes until pasta is tender but firm. Drain. Return to same pot. Cover to keep warm.

3 Tbsp (45 mL) butter

3 Tbsp (45 mL) all-purpose flour

1/2 tsp (2 mL) dried crushed chilies (optional)

1/4 tsp (1 mL) no-salt seasoning

2 1/2 cups (625 mL) milk

Melt butter in large saucepan on medium. Add next 3 ingredients. Heat and stir for 1 minute. Slowly add milk, stirring constantly until smooth. Heat and stir for about 5 minutes until boiling and thickened. Remove from heat.

2 cups (500 mL) grated light sharp Cheddar cheese

Add Cheddar cheese. Stir until smooth. Pour over pasta mixture. Stir until coated. Transfer to greased 3 quart (3 L) casserole.

1/3 cup (75 mL) fine dry bread crumbs (see Tip, page 86)

1/4 cup (60 mL) grated Parmesan cheese

2 Tbsp (30 mL) butter, melted

Combine remaining 3 ingredients in small bowl. Sprinkle over top. Bake in 350°F (175°C) oven for about 25 minutes until golden.

1 serving: 360 Calories; 16 g Total Fat (2 g Mono, 0 g Poly, 9 g Sat); 45 mg Cholesterol; 39 g Carbohydrate (3 g Fibre, 8 g Sugar); 18 g Protein; 440 mg Sodium

Rolled Eggplant Lasagna

Serves 2

Your very own personal vegetarian lasagna awaits you. Featuring tender marinated eggplant, custom balsamic tomato sauce and crunchy mozzarella. Easy to make in batches for the whole family.

2 lasagna noodles

2 Tbsp (30 mL) balsamic vinegar

2 tsp (10 mL) extra-virgin olive oil

1 tsp (5 mL) lemon juice

1/2 tsp (2 mL) paprika

1/4 tsp (1 mL) chopped fresh thyme

1/4 tsp (1 mL) pepper

1/2 eggplant, cut into 6 discs (1/2 inch, 12 mm, thick)

1/2 clove garlic, minced

1/2 cup (125 mL) tomato sauce

1 Tbsp (15 mL) balsamic vinegar

1 Tbsp (15 mL) lemon juice

1 Tbsp (15 mL) chopped fresh flat-leaf parsley

1/2 tsp (2 mL) paprika

1/4 tsp (1 mL) pepper

(see next page)

Cook lasagna noodles according to package directions. Transfer to parchment paper-lined baking sheet. Lay each noodle flat, not overlapping the other. Set aside.

On a large plate mix together next 6 ingredients to make a marinade. Add eggplant slices and turn to coat both sides. Heat a heavy-bottomed pan over high. Cook eggplant slices for 2 minutes on each side, until browned and softened but still able to hold shape. Set aside.

In a small bowl mix together next 7 ingredients. Sauce should be the consistency of yogurt; add water if necessary.

To assemble, cover 1 noodle entirely with a layer of tomato sauce mixture. Place 1 slice of eggplant in the centre. Top with half of red beans. Then fold one end of noodle over to cover. Place a spoonful of tomato sauce mixture on folded over noodle. Add 1 slice of eggplant. Top with half of cottage cheese. Fold other end of noodle over to cover. Place a spoonful of tomato sauce mixture on top. Add 1 slice of eggplant. Top with 1 slice of mozzarella cheese. Repeat process for second noodle. Bake for 10 minutes in 400°F (200°C) oven, then switch oven to high broil for 4 minutes to crisp top layer of cheese to a golden brown. Remove from oven. Let stand for 3 minutes.

Garnish with fresh basil.

1 serving: 360 Calories; 12 g Total Fat (5 g Mono, 0.5 g Poly, 4.5 g Sat); 15 mg Cholesterol; 45 g Carbohydrate (13 g Fibre, 10 g Sugar); 20 g Protein; 580 mg Sodium

2 × 1 oz (28 g) slices low-fat
mozzarella cheese

1/2 cup (125 mL) canned
red beans, rinsed

1/4 cup (125 mL) low-fat
cottage cheese

1/4 cup (60 mL) fresh basil

Tortilla Bake

Serves 6

A delicious layered dish using tortillas. Try the pesto or sun-dried tomato tortillas as an eye-catching alternative.

1 1/2 cups (375 mL) thick tomato pasta sauce (no salt added)

1 1/2 cups (375 mL) 1% cottage cheese

1 1/2 cups (375 mL) veggie ground round, lightly packed

6 whole-wheat flour tortillas (10 inch, 25 cm, diameter)

1/2 cup (125 mL) thick tomato pasta sauce (no salt added)

1 3/4 cups (425 mL) shredded mozzarella cheese

Combine first 3 ingredients in medium bowl.

To assemble, layer ingredients in greased 9 inch (23 cm) deep dish pie plate as follows:

1. 1 tortilla
2. Second amount of pasta sauce
3. 1 tortilla
4. 1/4 cottage cheese mixture
5. 1/4 cup (60 mL) mozzarella cheese
6. 1 tortilla
7. 1/4 cottage cheese mixture
8. 1/4 cup (60 mL) mozzarella cheese
9. 1 tortilla
10. 1/4 cottage cheese mixture
11. 1/4 cup (60 mL) mozzarella cheese
12. 1 tortilla
13. Remaining cottage cheese mixture
14. 1/4 cup (60 mL) mozzarella cheese
15. Remaining tortilla
16. Remaining mozzarella cheese

Place pie plate on baking sheet. Bake, uncovered, in 375°F (190°C) oven for about 45 minutes until cheese is melted and golden. Let stand for 10 minutes before serving. Cuts into 6 wedges.

1 serving: 360 Calories; 10 g Total Fat (0 g Mono, 0 g Poly, 4.5 g Sat); 20 mg Cholesterol; 40 g Carbohydrate (6 g Fibre, 7 g Sugar); 25 g Protein; 1100 mg Sodium

Spinach Cheese Pie

Serves 6

Spanokopita flavours abound in this appetizing pie. Buttery phyllo hides a cheesy spinach filling for a lovely and satisfying combination.

2 tsp (10 mL) cooking oil

1 cup (250 mL) chopped onion

2 large eggs, fork-beaten

2 × 10 oz (300 g) boxes of frozen chopped spinach, thawed and squeezed dry

1 cup (250 mL) crumbled feta cheese

3/4 cup (175 mL) ricotta cheese

3 Tbsp (45 mL) chopped fresh dill

1/4 tsp (1 mL) pepper

11 phyllo pastry sheets, thawed according to package directions

cooking spray

1/4 cup (60 mL) fine dry bread crumbs (see Tip, page 86)

Diagram

Heat cooking oil in medium frying pan on medium. Add onion. Cook for about 5 minutes, stirring often, until softened. Transfer to large bowl.

Add next 6 ingredients. Stir.

Place 1 pastry sheet on work surface. Cover remaining sheets with damp towel to prevent drying. Spray with cooking spray. Sprinkle with 1 1/2 tsp (7 mL) bread crumbs. Fold into thirds lengthwise to make a 4 inch (10 cm) strip. Repeat with 7 more pastry sheets, cooking spray and bread crumbs. Place 1 pastry strip in greased 9 inch (23 cm) deep dish pie plate, allowing ends of strip to hang over edge. Place second strip over first, at an angle and slightly overlapping. Repeat with remaining pastry strips until entire pie plate is covered (see Diagram). Gently press pastry to fit in pie plate, forming crust. Spray with cooking spray. Fill with spinach mixture. Spread evenly. Place 1 pastry sheet on work surface. Spray with cooking spray. Cover with 1 pastry sheet. Spray with cooking spray. Cover with remaining pastry sheet. Bunch up loosely. Place over spinach mixture. Bunch overhanging pastry toward centre of pie to cover. Spray with cooking spray. Bake on bottom rack in 350°F (175°C) oven for about 65 minutes until pastry is browned and internal temperature reaches 165°F (74°C). Let stand on wire rack for 10 minutes. Cuts into 6 wedges.

1 serving: 350 Calories; 12 g Total Fat (3.5 g Mono, 1 g Poly, 6 g Sat); 100 mg Cholesterol; 39 g Carbohydrate (5 g Fibre, 6 g Sugar); 18 g Protein; 770 mg Sodium

Indy Shepherd's Pie

Serves 2

A recreation of a classic into a personalized vegetarian pie. Enjoy the flavours of sweet corn and creamy mashed potato with a crunchy bite of quinoa.

2 medium russet potatoes, washed and patted dry

2 tsp (10 mL) extra-virgin olive oil

1/8 tsp (0.5 mL) salt

1/2 tsp (2 mL) pepper

1 tsp (5 mL) unsalted butter

1 clove garlic, minced

1/2 onion, diced

1/2 cup (125 mL) frozen corn, thawed

1/3 cup (75 mL) cooked red quinoa

2 Tbsp (30 mL) tomato paste (see Tip, page 38)

1 tsp (5 mL) chopped fresh Italian parsley

1/2 tsp (2 mL) paprika

1/8 tsp (0.5 mL) ground nutmeg

1/8 tsp (0.5 mL) salt

1/4 tsp (1 mL) pepper

Coat both potatoes with olive oil, then sprinkle with salt and pepper and wrap individually in foil. Place on bottom rack of 425°F (220°C) oven and bake for 45 minutes or until potatoes are soft. Test by squeezing lightly with fingers; if the potatoes give to light pressure, they are ready. Remove from oven, partially unwrap foil and set aside.

Heat a large heavy-bottomed frying pan over medium-high. Add first amount of butter and heat until melted. Add garlic, onion and corn and cook, stirring, until onion begins to soften, about 2 minutes.

Reduce heat to medium. Stir in next 7 ingredients. Cook for 3 minutes. Remove from heat and set aside.

Slice a sliver off the long side of each potato. Using a small spoon, hollow out each potato, leaving a shell approximately 1/2 inch (12 mm) thick. Transfer removed potato to a medium saucepan over medium-high. Add next 3 ingredients. Whip vigorously to a smooth consistency; add more milk if necessary. Transfer whipped potato to small piping bag or resealable plastic bag with corner snipped off.

To construct, pipe a small amount of potato into bottom of 1 shell. Cover with half of corn mixture, followed by 2 Tbsp (30 mL) of cheese. Pipe mashed potato over cheese to heap out of potato shell. Sprinkle with 1 Tbsp (15 mL) cheese. Repeat with second potato shell. Return to 425°F (220°C) oven for 8 minutes. Remove from oven. Let stand for 2 minutes before serving.

1 serving: 370 Calories; 11 g Total Fat (4 g Mono, 0.5 g Poly, 4 g Sat); 15 mg Cholesterol; 60 g Carbohydrate (7 g Fibre, 8 g Sugar); 13 g Protein; 610 mg Sodium

1/4 cup (60 mL) milk

1 tsp (5 mL) unsalted butter

1/8 tsp (0.5 mL) salt

6 Tbsp (90 mL) shredded
Cheddar cheese

Polenta Vegetable Stacks

Serves 4

Plenty of polenta piled high with sauteed vegetables makes for fast, fresh comfort food. Add a dash of hot sauce if you like. You can store extra polenta, tightly wrapped, in the fridge for up to one month.

1 Tbsp (15 mL) olive oil

1/2 × 2.2 lbs (1 kg) polenta roll, cut into 8 rounds

8 slices jalapeño Monterey Jack cheese (about 3 oz, 85 g)

1 Tbsp (15 mL) olive oil

1 1/2 cups (375 mL) thinly sliced zucchini (with peel)

2 cloves garlic, minced

1 × 14 oz (398 mL) can of diced tomatoes (no salt added), drained

1 cup (250 mL) canned black beans, rinsed and drained

8 slices jalapeño Monterey Jack cheese (about 3 oz, 85 g)

lime wedges, for garnish

Heat first amount of olive oil in large frying pan on medium-high. Add polenta. Cook for about 2 minutes per side until golden. Transfer to greased 9 × 13 inch (23 × 33 cm) baking dish.

Place slice of cheese on each polenta round. Cover to keep warm.

Heat second amount of olive oil in same frying pan on medium. Add zucchini and garlic. Cook for about 3 minutes, stirring occasionally, until zucchini is tender-crisp.

Add tomatoes and beans. Cook for about 1 minute until heated through. Spoon over polenta. Top with second amount of cheese slices. Broil on centre rack in oven for about 2 minutes until cheese is melted.

Garnish with lime wedges. Makes 8 stacks.

1 serving: 370 Calories; 19 g Total Fat (4.5 g Mono, 0.5 g Poly, 8 g Sat); 40 mg Cholesterol; 32 g Carbohydrate (5 g Fibre, 5 g Sugar); 17 g Protein; 850 mg Sodium

Unrolled Maki

Serves 2

A new take on a maki roll using crisped sushi rice, chanterelle mushrooms, swiss chard and cucumber. Enjoy a wide range of nutrients with this nifty deconstruction.

1/2 cup (125 mL) medium-grain white rice, rinsed

1/2 cup (125 mL) water

Combine rice and water in medium saucepan over medium. Bring to a boil, reduce heat to low and simmer, covered, until water is absorbed, about 20 minutes. Remove from heat.

1 green onion, thinly sliced

1 tsp (5 mL) rice wine vinegar

1/8 tsp (0.5 mL) salt

Stir in green onion, first amount of vinegar and salt. Spread rice flat on a plate and place in refrigerator to cool completely, about 1 hour.

Shape cooled rice into 2 equal-sized balls, then squish them down to form round discs about 3/4 inch (20 mm) thick. Coat rice discs with bread crumbs.

1/4 cup (60 mL) fine dry bread crumbs (see Tip, page 86)

Heat a heavy-bottomed frying pan over high. Add first amount of butter and heat until melted. Add mushrooms. Cook until they begin to brown, then add second amount of vinegar, no-salt seasoning and pepper. Stir. Transfer mushroom mixture to a small bowl. Set aside.

2 tsp (10 mL) butter

1/2 cup (125 mL) chopped chanterelle mushrooms

1/2 tsp (2 mL) rice wine vinegar

1/8 tsp (0.5 mL) no-salt seasoning

1/8 tsp (0.5 mL) pepper

Return pan to stove over medium. Add swiss chard and garlic. Cook until chard begins to wilt, then add soy sauce and wasabi powder. Stir. Discard crushed garlic. Transfer to another small bowl and set aside.

2 large leaves swiss chard, cut into bite-sized pieces

1 clove garlic, crushed

1 Tbsp (15 mL) low-sodium soy sauce

1/2 tsp (2 mL) wasabi powder

(see next page)

Return pan to stove over medium-high. Add second amount of butter and heat until melted. Gently place rice cakes in pan and cook until bottoms are golden brown and crispy. Flip rice cakes, then top with chard mixture, followed by mushroom mixture. Transfer entire pan to 400°F (200°C) oven for 6 minutes.

Garnish rice cakes with avocado, cucumber, nori and alfalfa sprouts.

1 serving: 380 Calories; 16 g Total Fat (7 g Mono, 1.5 g Poly, 6 g Sat); 20 mg Cholesterol; 53 g Carbohydrate (6 g Fibre, 3 g Sugar); 8 g Protein; 630 mg Sodium

2 tsp (10 mL) butter

1/2 avocado, thinly sliced

1/4 English cucumber, cut julienne

1/2 sheet nori, sliced into thin strips

1/2 cup (125 mL) alfalfa sprouts

Market Mushroom

Serves 2

Reminiscent of a classic French stew, this dish also provides you with a generous diversity of vitamins and minerals.

4 large portobello mushrooms, stems and gills removed

1 tsp (5 mL) extra-virgin olive oil

1 tsp (5 mL) lemon juice

1/4 tsp (1 mL) chopped fresh thyme

1/8 tsp (0.5 mL) salt

1/4 tsp (1 mL) pepper

1 Tbsp (15 mL) extra-virgin olive oil

1/2 cup (125 mL) diced red onion

3/4 cup (175 mL) diced red pepper

3/4 cup (175 mL) diced zucchini

3/4 cup (175 mL) diced eggplant

1 clove garlic, minced

1/4 cup (60 mL) fine dry bread crumbs (see Tip, page 86)

3 Tbsp (45 mL) tomato paste (see Tip, page 38)

2 Tbsp (30 mL) dry white wine

(see next page)

Cut 2 mushrooms into a small dice. Transfer to a small bowl and set aside. Place 2 remaining mushrooms on baking sheet. Combine next 5 ingredients and drizzle over mushrooms. Bake in 400°F (200°C) oven for 12 to 14 minutes, until mushrooms begin to soften. Remove from oven. Tent with foil. Set aside.

Heat a large heavy-bottomed pan over high. Add second amount of olive oil. Add diced mushroom to pan and cook for 2 to 3 minutes or until mushroom begins to brown. Add onion and red pepper to pan and continue to cook for 2 minutes. Then add zucchini, eggplant and garlic; cook for another 2 to 3 minutes, until all vegetables have begun to sweat.

Stir in next 7 ingredients. Reduce heat. Cover and simmer for 5 minutes.

Scoop mixture generously into par-baked mushroom caps and return to 400°F (200°C) oven for 5 minutes. Scoop any leftover filling onto plates. Top with baked mushrooms. Garnish with basil and goat cheese.

1 serving: 370 Calories; 17 g Total Fat (9 g Mono, 1 g Poly, 4 g Sat); trace Cholesterol; 43 g Carbohydrate (8 g Fibre, 20 g Sugar); 15 g Protein; 700 mg Sodium

1 Tbsp (15 mL) red wine
vinegar

1 sprig fresh thyme,
chopped

2 tsp (10 mL) brown sugar

1/8 tsp (0.5 mL) salt

1/4 cup (60 mL) chopped
fresh basil

3 oz (85 g) goat cheese

Arriba Mushroom

Serves 2

Mexican flavours of black bean, corn and oregano, topped with a cool yogurt. Well balanced and packed with vegetarian protein.

2 large portobello mushrooms, stems and gills removed

1 tsp (5 mL) extra-virgin olive oil

1 tsp (5 mL) lemon juice

1 tsp (5 mL) chopped fresh Italian parsley

1/8 tsp (0.5 mL) salt

1/4 tsp (1 mL) pepper

1 cup (250 mL) water

3/4 cup (175 mL) diced potato

1 Tbsp (15 mL) butter

3/4 cup (175 mL) canned black beans

1/2 cup (125 mL) diced zucchini

1/4 cup (60 mL) frozen corn, thawed

1/4 tsp (1 mL) salt

1 tsp (5 mL) chili powder

1/4 cup (60 mL) Greek yogurt

1 Tbsp (15 mL) lemon juice

2 tsp (10 mL) liquid honey

1/2 tsp (2 mL) chopped fresh oregano

1/2 tsp (2 mL) paprika

Place mushrooms on baking sheet. Combine next 5 ingredients and drizzle over mushrooms. Bake in 400°F (200°C) oven for 10 to 12 minutes, until mushrooms begin to soften. Remove from oven. Tent with foil. Set aside.

Heat a large heavy-bottomed pan over high. Add water and potato and boil for 5 minutes. Strain off water and return pan with potatoes to stove over medium-high. Add butter and cook until potato begins to brown and soften. Stir in beans, zucchini, corn, salt and chili powder. Reduce heat to medium and cook for 2 to 3 minutes. Scoop mixture generously into mushroom caps. Bake in 400°F (200°C) oven for 10 minutes.

Mix together remaining 5 ingredients in small bowl; transfer to piping bag or resealable plastic bag with corner snipped off. Pipe yogurt mixture over stuffed mushrooms. Serve with any leftover filling.

1 serving: 350 Calories; 13 g Total Fat (3.5 g Mono, 0.5 g Poly, 6 g Sat); 25 mg Cholesterol; 51 g Carbohydrate (8 g Fibre, 13 g Sugar); 13 g Protein; 720 mg Sodium

Zucchini Hercules

Serves 2

Vegetables of the Mediterranean stuffed into a herb-infused zucchini and baked with Havarti. Loaded with enough vitamins and minerals to make you feel like Hercules. Great as a main dish or sliced and placed on taster spoons for an intriguing appetizer.

2 large zucchini

1 Tbsp (15 mL) extra-virgin olive oil

1 tsp (5 mL) lemon juice

1/4 tsp (1 mL) chopped fresh thyme

1/4 tsp (1 mL) paprika

1/8 tsp (0.5 mL) salt

1/4 tsp (1 mL) pepper

1 Tbsp (15 mL) canola oil

6 fresh mushrooms, diced

2 Tbsp (30 mL) dry white wine

1 clove garlic, minced

1/2 red onion, diced

1/2 red pepper, diced

4 olives, pitted and diced

1/8 tsp (0.5 mL) salt

1/8 tsp (0.5 mL) pepper

1/2 cup (125 mL) fine dry bread crumbs (see Tip, page 86)

1/4 cup (60 mL) grated jalapeño Havarti cheese

Remove both ends from both zucchini, then slice each one in half vertically. Using a melon baller, scoop shallow holes down length of each zucchini half, leaving a 1/2 inch (12 mm) gap between each hole. Transfer zucchini scoops to cutting board and dice, then set aside.

Place zucchini halves onto foil-lined baking sheet. Sprinkle with next 6 ingredients. Bake in 375°F (190°C) oven for 12 minutes, or until zucchini begins to soften. Remove and set aside to cool.

Heat a heavy-bottomed pan over high. Add canola oil and heat for 1 minute. Add mushrooms and cook until browned, 2 to 3 minutes. Stir in white wine. Cook until all wine is evaporated.

Add diced zucchini and next 6 ingredients. Continue to cook, stirring, until vegetables just begin to sweat, about 1 minute. Remove from heat. Stir in bread crumbs.

Spoon mixture generously into zucchini halves. Top with cheese. Bake in 400°F (200°C) oven for 8 to 10 minutes, until cheese begins to brown. Remove from oven. Let stand for 3 to 4 minutes. Serve with any leftover filling.

1 serving: 400 Calories; 23 g Total Fat (12 g Mono, 3.5 g Poly, 6 g Sat); 20 mg Cholesterol; 39 g Carbohydrate (7 g Fibre, 11 g Sugar); 13 g Protein; 640 mg Sodium

Miso Lettuce Cups

Serves 2

Crisp lettuce cups stuffed with a crunchy savoury vegetable blend. An excellent interactive meal that supplies well-balanced nutrition.

2 tsp (10 mL) cooking oil

3/4 cup (175 mL) carrot, cut julienne

3 button mushrooms, thinly sliced

2 green onions, thinly sliced

1 cup (250 mL) chopped napa cabbage

1/2 cup (125 mL) fresh edamame beans

2 Tbsp (30 mL) water

4 tsp (20 mL) miso paste

1 Tbsp (15 mL) molasses

1 tsp (5 mL) rice wine vinegar

1/8 tsp (0.5 mL) cayenne pepper

1/2 cup (125 mL) chow mein noodles

2 Tbsp (30 mL) peanuts

1 small head iceberg lettuce

1 Tbsp (15 mL) chopped fresh cilantro

Heat a heavy-bottomed frying pan over high. Add cooking oil and heat for 1 minute. Add carrot and mushroom and cook for 1 to 2 minutes, until carrot begins to soften. Add onion, cabbage and edamame. Reduce heat to medium. Continue to cook, stirring, for another 2 minutes or until cabbage has started to wilt.

Combine next 5 ingredients in small bowl, then stir into cabbage mixture.

Add noodles and peanuts; gently stir to distribute evenly and coat with sauce.

Slice iceberg lettuce into 2 halves from top to bottom. Remove and discard stem and core of lettuce. Gently pull apart lettuce cups. Fill cups with mixture. Garnish with cilantro.

1 serving: 380 Calories; 16 g Total Fat (6 g Mono, 4 g Poly, 2 g Sat); 0 mg Cholesterol; 49 g Carbohydrate (11 g Fibre, 19 g Sugar); 16 g Protein; 590 mg Sodium

Index